SONGBIRDS
How to Attract Them and Identify Their Songs

SONGBIRDS
How to Attract Them and Identify Their Songs

NOBLE PROCTOR PhD

Rodale Press, Emmaus, Pennsylvania

A QUARTO BOOK

Copyright © 1988 Quarto Publishing plc

Published in 1988 in the United States of America by
Rodale Press, Inc.
33 East Minor Street
Emmaus, PA 18049

Reprinted 1990

ISBN 0-87857-773-4

This book was designed and produced by
Quarto Publishing plc
The Old Brewery
6 Blundell Street
London N7 9BH

Project Editor: David Black
Senior Editor: Kate Kirby

Designer: Hazel Edington

Bird Artist: David Ord Kerr
Illustrator: Vana Haggerty
Chart Composition: Elly King

Art Director: Moira Clinch
Editorial Director: Carolyn King

Typeset by Text Filmsetters Ltd, London
Manufactured in Hong Kong by Regent Publishing Services Limited
Printed by Lee Fung-Asco Printers Ltd, Hong Kong

CONTENTS

INTRODUCTION

BIRDS, MORE THAN ANY OTHER living creatures, have perfected the production of vocal sounds. The songs of birds are a great pleasure to man, inspiring both poetry and music linked with thoughts of spring.

Bird sounds can be heard on every continent, but not all their vocalizations can be called songs. Short and simple noises are commonly known as calls, and can be produced by both male and female at any time of year. Songs are more complex, and are usually produced by the male during the breeding season.

Of the 8,500 to 9,000 bird species in the world, one particular group is noted for its ability to sing – the oscines, or songbirds. These form 80 percent of the order Passeriformes, which itself comprises more than 5,000 species of perching birds, or passerines, which range in size from small flycatchers to large crows, and includes larks, nightingales, thrushes, warblers, and finches. The remaining passerines are known as sub-oscines, and include the tyrant flycatchers, cotingas, antbirds, and woodcreepers of the New World, and the Old World pittas and lyrebirds.

Songbirds are aptly named for the sheer complexity of the songs they render, many of which are impossible to describe in words. They *can* be called warbling, twittering, trilling, rattling, or whistling, or fluty, sweet, mellow, shrill, rich, or liquid; but no combination of these words can truly evoke the sound.

The quality of song as we hear it differs widely among the songbirds, and what delights one person may not appeal to another. Certain species stand out, of course, and have provided inspiration to both music and literature. Of European birds, the nightingale

An Eastern meadowlark (above) sings its sweet song from a fence post perch.

"Fluent and wistful" are two adjectives used to describe the song of the European willow warbler shown singing in a gorse bush (left).

A male European blackbird (top) shown in sleek breeding plumage.

An African rufous-naped lark (above) sings from the top of a thorn tree.

inspires more myths and poetry than any other, perhaps the best-known poem being Keats' "Ode to a Nightingale." The songs of blackbird, song thrush, and skylark have also been immortalized in verse. The repetition of a mockingbird's song is incorporated into Walt Whitman's "Out of the Cradle Endlessly Rocking," and poems by the ornithologist Alexander Wilson describe many birds. In music, the nightingale makes frequent appearances, as does the cuckoo, in works by Beethoven, Haydn, Vivaldi, Liszt, and Grieg. European goldfinch, linnet, barn swallow, and the European robin can be heard in a number of musical works, and if you listen carefully to Dvořák's *American String Quartet* you can hear a scarlet tanager. The complexity of birds' songs makes their translation into music difficult, but one twentieth-century composer, Oliver Messiaen, has incorporated the songs or calls of 260 species from all over the world into 10 of his major works.

Almost concealed from view, a winter wren (right) sings in an elderberry bush. For their small size wrens have loud and penetrating songs.

Courtship of the common Asian iora (right) includes an acrobatic songflight in which the bird makes a sharp ascent and sings as it spirals slowly down.

A male reed bunting (left) in boldly marked spring plumage at its song perch in a willow thicket.

As the year progresses the bird song around us changes. Many of the first spring visitors are heard before they are seen, and the sudden addition of their songs to the sounds around us is always a source of great pleasure. Although song is merely a product of the reproductive urge, it seems to communicate much more. Spring bird song is part of the reawakening from winter, and the emotions it can generate in us make it easy to imagine the birds are singing for sheer joy.

Reasons to sing

The question of why some birds sing well and others don't is closely linked with their evolution and the need to sing. Habitat plays an important part. In an enclosed environment – such as a forest where visual signals are difficult – loud song is essential for communication. A good example of this is the far-carrying tones of the South American bellbird. Forests contain a high proportion of highly vocal species, and shelter some of the world's finest songbirds. Reedbeds and dense bushes are other closed habitats, and the warblers and wrens which live there all have loud songs. In a more open habitat, such as tundra or plains, birds can use visual displays more effectively; aerial songs here more commonly serve to draw attention to the display.

An analysis of those birds which primarily use song to communicate showed they tend to be small in size; have plumage which blends with their environment; use simple visual displays; live in a more enclosed habitat; have a marked territorial instinct; and are solitary breeders. Few birds show all these characteristics, but most songbirds show at least some of them.

INTERNATIONAL SONGSTERS

THE AFRICAN PLAINS are home to many birds sporting bright colors or elaborate plumage, both of which take the place of complex songs as a method of communication. Thus, widowbirds have displays which make the most of their long tails and bright plumage; many of the chats have colored wing patches and display dances; and the starling species use their iridescent colors to great effect. These birds usually have harsh songs, which serve solely to attract a female to the more dramatic visual display. Move to the tropical forests of Africa, however, and song becomes the predominant means of communication. One family of songsters includes the bulbuls and greenbuls, which are generally an uninspiring gray, green, brown, and yellow. The robin chats, another family of outstanding singers, live in dense forest undergrowth and all have similar appearance, with orange-red underparts and a grayish back. The bou-bous, members of the shrike family, live in dense thickets and woodland, and have evolved intricate song duets between male and female.

In Australia the same pattern is followed, with less musical birds in open country and the finest singers inhabiting the forests. Australia is home to some of the most brightly colored finches – like the Gouldian finch, blue-faced finch, and crimson finch – none of which has songs worth mentioning. In the forests there is a chorus of songs from pied butcherbirds, babblers, whistlers, and honeyeaters, as well as scrubwrens in the dense undergrowth. The best mimics in Australia must be the lyrebirds, which are brown, chicken-sized birds that live in the rainforest. To make up for their dull colors they have an extremely loud song in which they imitate the songs of other forest birds, combining them with their display, which makes use of their exceptional tail-feathers. The outer tail feathers of the male superb lyrebird are lyre-shaped and composed of alternate bands of light and dark-colored feathers. The remaining tail feathers are delicate filaments.

When the male bird reaches the climax of its vocal renderings, the display is dramatically reinforced by the tail feathers being flipped over the head, the fine ones being vibrated to form a shimmering veil which both entices and then engulfs the receptive female.

Rüppell's robin chat (above), one of East Africa's finest singers, has a warbling song and also mimics other species. It is a shy bird, found in dense upland forest, where it sings from thick cover.

One of New Zealand's best forest singers is the bellbird (above) which can be heard throughout the year. It has a number of different songs and at a distance some of the notes sound remarkably bell-like.

Sometimes known as bellbird, the bell miner of Australia (above right) lives in rain forest and gives a clear single note which varies in pitch. A group of them produce a pleasant tinkling sound.

A pair of red-eyed bulbuls (right) display aggressively to each other. Their loud and fluty song, typical of the family, can be heard coming from riverside bushes in southern Africa.

As a contrast, the birds of paradise, which mainly inhabit New Guinea, have what is possibly the most brightly colored and ornate plumage of all birds. Their displays show off their plumes to the best advantage, and may even involve hanging upside-down. Their songs are disappointing, however, often just a soft warble.

Central and South America have more forested areas than perhaps anywhere else in the world. The tropical climate of much of it means there is little migration, as food is available year-round, and birds can successfully breed at almost any time of year. The dense rain forests can be divided into layers, with different species occupying each. Many birds on the forest floor, where little light penetrates and the ground is often open, are outstanding singers, such as the nightingale-thrushes. The numerous species of antbirds, though classed as sub-oscines, still have loud and, sometimes, musical songs. Most of the wrens – which live in forest undergrowth and thickets, and are generally brown and skulking – are superb singers, with many of them duetting as a pair. Other members of the thrush family are among the world's best feathered singers, with the slate-colored solitaire ranking at the top.

In the forest and thick scrub of Asia, the most vociferous birds include bulbuls; babblers (especially the hwamei, a vocal and musical laughing-thrush); thrushes, like the shamas, and robins; and flycatchers and warblers; many of these birds can only be identified by their songs.

A European sedge warbler (right) sings from the top of a flowering gorse bush. It produces a rapid medley of notes and like its relative the marsh warbler, incorporates the songs of very many other birds.

A red-throated pipit (above) calls, camouflaged against grasses near its tundra nest site.

The woodland species of Europe contain some excellent singers. The nightingale, in particular, illustrates the link between song and habitat well, being a basically nondescript brown bird which habitually skulks in thick vegetation. Its song is not only complex but extremely loud and an inspiration to poets and musicians alike. All European thrushes are good singers, perhaps the least musical being the ring ousel, which breeds in open upland hills and mountains and has a much shorter song phrase than its relatives. European warblers are mainly small brown birds which live in woodland, scrub, or reedbeds, and have a delightful range of songs. Some, like the sedge warbler and the whitethroat, also have a song flight. The pipits also have song flights and complex songs, though nothing to rival that of the skylark.

No two bird species have exactly the same song, and wherever you travel there will always be new songs to hear. Various species earn the title of best singer in different countries. In Europe, it is arguably the nightingale, or perhaps the skylark, although some prefer the songs of the closely related woodlark and

thrush nightingale; in North America, the hermit and wood thrushes and mockingbird take precedence; in South and Central America, the slate-colored solitaire; in Asia, the shama and the Pekin robin; in Australia, the superb lyrebird and pied butcherbird; in New Zealand, the bellbird and tui; and in Africa, the robin-chats, especially the white-browed species.

Many birds are caged and bred as a result of their singing ability, a practice which dates back to the Ancient Greeks. Finches of various types have proved the most popular as they are easily fed; one species, the canary, is now bred in a truly bewildering variety of plumages. The large-scale trapping of birds for the cagebird market still goes on around the world, and millions of birds are trapped each year; sadly, a high proportion of these die before they are even sold. Many countries have introduced tight controls on the export and import of birds, but many species – especially parrots – are seriously threatened by the trade.

The wood thrush (top) is one of North America's best songsters, with an unhurried, liquid, bell-like melody.

A mockingbird (above) shown here at the edge of a Florida swamp, lives in a variety of habitats throughout North America.

WHY BIRDS SING

A male red-winged blackbird (left) defines its territory with its loud gurgling song, at the same time exposing its bright red epaulets.

WHEN LISTENING TO A BIRD'S SONG it is often tempting to interpret its reasons for singing in solely human terms. Bird song gives us pleasure, but from the birds' point of view it is an entirely functional form of communication. Singing is directed at members of a bird's own species, and it follows that each species has a different song, while individuals of each species sound alike. However, there is an occasional variation between different populations of the same species, in the form of dialects, which can distinguish subspecies.

In general it is the male which sings, although the females of some species can also sing, though usually not as well. Males use song to draw attention to themselves, whereas females in the vulnerable position of incubating eggs or young want to remain hidden.

Establishing home boundaries

One of the prime reasons for bird song is to establish the existence and boundaries of a territory. It is within this territory that a pair of birds will raise their young, so it must be jealously guarded from rivals as it will provide food and protection for both parents and young until the breeding season is complete. Singing lets other males of the same species know that a family is in residence and that intruders are not welcome. The song means nothing to different species, but as these will often have different food and nesting requirements anyway, a singer on its territory will ignore their presence, just as they in turn ignore his. Within a given territory it is possible to have robin, cardinal, catbird, and yellowthroat all nesting without interfering with each other's needs.

The male chooses a series of song posts from which to sing and by singing from each of them regularly he can define his territory. The borders are invisible, of course, but if ever a rival male crosses into an occupied territory he will be instantly challenged by the occupant. The ensuing fights or chases may sometimes involve aggressive bursts of song to help see off the intruder. The territory's original "owner" invariably emerges as the winner of such disputes. Some cunning birds have an entire repertoire of songs, and use a different one at each song post. This may well create the illusion of a number of occupied territories, and thus be more successful at keeping would-be intruders away.

Effective advertising

Another use for bird song is to advertise to a female that there is an unattached male present who is offering her a home. It follows, then, that a male who is paired up

will tend to sing less, using his song purely for territorial reasons, though how a female can distinguish between the songs of a bachelor bird and one which is happily paired is not clear. Singing also serves to strengthen the bond between a pair, and may also be involved with further courtship leading to mating.

Some birds may also have a sub-song, often a quieter and lower version of their normal song. It does not carry for any distance and is usually heard only in fall and early spring. Some sub-songs are almost certainly rendered by young birds which have not yet reached the stage of full territorial singing, and could therefore be regarded as a form of practicing.

Another form of song is a type of excited outburst which happens at random and contains many improvised elements, unlike the stereotyped territorial song. The outburst may be delivered from a perched position, but is more often given in an "ecstasy flight"; it has been suggested that this sort of song may be a form of emotional release. The outburst usually occurs at the peak of the breeding season, often at night or twilight. Mockingbirds, yellowthroats, and ovenbirds are some species that regularly indulge.

Bird calls are functionally different from songs, and so have a different structure. They are short simple sounds, usually of one or two syllables. Some are more complex, however, and almost fall into the song category, just as some songs are simple and – by the human ear, at least – could be mistaken for calls. Calls, however, communicate totally different messages from songs.

The European robin (above) sings throughout the year from both open and well-concealed posts. It is extremely aggressive and territorial.

Starlings and house sparrows (right) coexist in man-made built-up areas. Starlings tend to feed on insect larvae and worms and berries, while sparrows take mainly soft-bodied insects and seeds.

A flock of male and female chaffinches (above) feed on grain. In spring a loud call is used by young birds to find unoccupied territories and when selecting suitable song posts.

A fieldfare (left) displays aggression towards a starling. Loud calls often form part of such displays which in this case relate to possession of an apple but could equally be over territory.

A variety of calls

Songbirds tend to have a larger repertoire of calls than other birds, many having a vocabulary of 20 or more calls. Calls may be used to communicate with a partner, to beg for food, to call young birds, to keep contact with members of the same species within a flock, to show aggression, or to signal that a predator is near.

Once the male's song has attracted a mate, calling between pairs often forms part of the courtship ritual. Courtship feeding by the male is usually accompanied by a begging call from the female, a sound similar to that used by young birds when trying to elicit food from their parents. Parent birds can call young birds to them when they have scattered after leaving the nest, particularly useful for precocial species (mobile before they are fully grown). Migrating birds call to one another when flying in a flock, a practice which enables a nocturnal migrant to rejoin the flock if it becomes separated. Feeding flocks in woodland call constantly; this helps them to forage more effectively, and enables them to signal when they locate a food source. Winter flocks of birds like chickadees have foraging territories which may be defended from other flocks. This is particularly important in times of food shortage, when each member of the flock will identify themselves by a call. If an individual who does not belong to the flock – and who therefore has a different call – enters the foraging area, it is immediately spotted and driven away. Threat calls form part of aggression displays when a territorial male is fighting off an intruder.

Perhaps the most interesting type of call is the one which alerts birds to the presence of a predator. The alarm call has the same basic pattern for a wide range of species. It is a short, high-pitched note which can be heard clearly, but gives little information about the location of the calling bird. This call usually results in all of the small birds taking cover, and is given when a bird of prey is spotted nearby. A different type of alarm call will be sounded if a stationary predator is seen; owls usually provoke this type of call if they are discovered roosting. Instead of a short, high note, a loud scolding type of call, repeated many times, draws attention. This sound is interpreted by other species who usually come to investigate before joining in. The resulting chorus of scolding noises is part of a mobbing display, and the birds will often approach very close to the object of their attention. If the owl moves, the short, high call is given and all dive for cover. Mobbing usually persuades the target of the outburst to move on.

Its wings spread and tail fanned, a nightingale (left) sings its legendary song from deep undergrowth. It gives a harsh scolding call when alarmed, and also a sweeter note used as a contact call.

HOW BIRDS SING

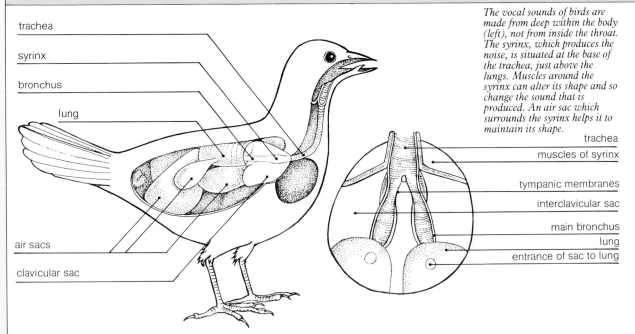

trachea

syrinx

bronchus

lung

air sacs

clavicular sac

The vocal sounds of birds are made from deep within the body (left), not from inside the throat. The syrinx, which produces the noise, is situated at the base of the trachea, just above the lungs. Muscles around the syrinx can alter its shape and so change the sound that is produced. An air sac which surrounds the syrinx helps it to maintain its shape.

trachea

muscles of syrinx

tympanic membranes

interclavicular sac

main bronchus

lung

entrance of sac to lung

THE VOCAL SOUNDS PRODUCED by birds are made in a completely different manner to those produced by mammals. Instead of having a larynx with vocal cords situated at the top of the trachea, birds possess an organ called the syrinx. This is a V-shaped structure situated at the base of the trachea (windpipe) where it divides into two bronchi that run to the lungs. Inside the syrinx are thin tympanic membranes which vibrate when air passes over them as it escapes from the lungs. The shape of the syrinx can be altered by muscles attached to it. This in turn changes the shape and tension of the tympanic membranes, which then varies the pitch of the sound produced. The more muscles to control the syrinx, the richer the range of sound. The principle can be illustrated by blowing up a balloon full of air and then stretching the neck of the balloon as the air escapes: the more the neck is stretched, the higher the sound. Vultures have none of these muscles, geese have only one pair, hummingbirds have two, and parrots have three. Songbirds have from five to nine which give them their wide vocal abilities.

VARIATIONS ON A THEME

OF THE SONGBIRDS, the ovenbirds, woodcreepers, and antbirds (the sub-oscines) have the most primitive type of syrinx, with the membranes attached only to the trachea. The rest of the songbirds have mem-

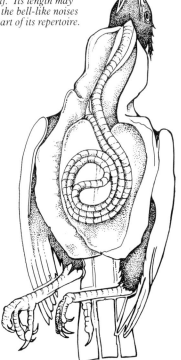

The trachea of the trumpet bird (right) from New Guinea and Australia is so long that it coils round on itself. Its length may help to make the bell-like noises which form part of its repertoire.

branes which can be attached to both the trachea and the bronchi in a variety of ways.

Part of a bird's respiratory system is formed by a series of air sacs; these allow a greater volume of air to be taken in than the lungs alone would hold. The interclavicular air sac surrounds the syrinx and exerts pressure on it. This particular air sac is essential for the production of sounds; if ruptured, no sounds can be made. The trachea can also play a role in sound-making, by acting as a resonance chamber.

Among the different bird species, there is a great variation in syrinx structure and, therefore, the types of sound produced. Wood and hermit thrushes can use the two branches of the syrinx independently, producing two notes at the same time. This accounts for the flute-like and two-tone quality of their songs.

The length and width of the trachea also play a part in the final sound. A short, narrow trachea produces a higher resonance than does a short, broad trachea. The trumpetbird, a bird of paradise, has the top and base of its trachea only three or three and a half inches apart, and the trachea, about 20 inches long, coils around on itself. As song originates from the base of the trachea, it is possible for birds to sing with their bills full of food, or even closed.

The aptly named Amazonian umbrella-bird (above) displays a large scarlet air sac when it calls. This enables it to produce a prolonged low bellowing sound which resembles distant cattle.

Large "sacs" or tympani, formed from an enlarged esophagus, act as resonance chambers for the greater prairie chicken (left). They are largest in the male, who inflates them during courtship amplifying his booming call. It can be heard more than a mile away.

European woodcock

Woodpeckers communicate over large distances by hammering with their beaks on dead trunks and boughs. The European great spotted woodpecker (right) produces a rapid, resonating drumming sound. The outer primary feathers of woodcocks (far right) have been converted into effective sound vibrators. During their courtship flights the vibrating feathers make a high whistling sound.

Great spotted woodpecker

Tail feathers

Unusual sounds

Some species, not noted for their songs, use their air sacs to produce extraordinary sounds. Greater and lesser prairie chickens inflate theirs to produce a booming sound, and the sacs can be seen stretching the bare neck skin as they are inflated. Pigeons inflate their esophagus with air to give their characteristic cooing tone. The modification of syrinx, trachea, and air sacs is what makes bird song and sounds so beautifully varied and unique.

Many birds – though relatively few songbirds – produce sounds other than vocal noises by using parts of their bodies. The low thumping and drumming of the ruffed grouse is produced when it fans its wings to trap air next to its body. Hummingbirds are so-called because of the noise their wings make, and the varying species each produce a different hum. Wing clapping occurs in the display of some pigeons. Common nighthawks produce a booming sound with their primaries. The woodcock has specially modified primaries which whistle. Of the songbirds, manakins make use of wing noises in their displays, producing a variety of loud snapping and whirring noises, while flappet larks also generate wing sounds.

Other parts of the body can be used to produce sounds. Storks clap their bills together to make a loud rattling sound, and woodpeckers drum with their bills against a tree or branch. Snipe produce a drumming or winnowing sound with their outer tail feathers, and one songbird – the lyre-tailed honeyguide – is thought to make a sound with its outer tail feathers, as well.

Learning songs

Just how much of a bird's singing ability is inherited and how much is learned was one question asked by early ornithologists. In the early eighteenth century, Baron Ferdinand von Pernau observed that if a young bird never hears the song of its parent it does not develop its full natural song. More recent experiments have shown this to be true, though the Baron was only partly correct when he also concluded that these young birds would learn the song of any other species that was put with them.

When a bird is isolated from the influence of its

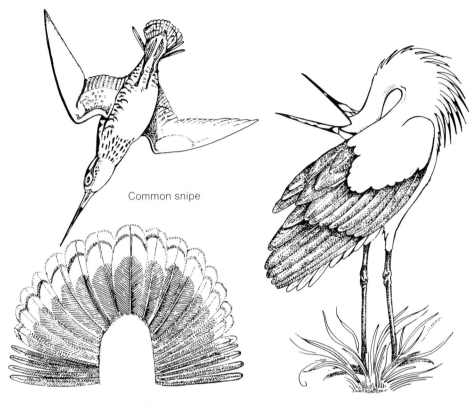

Common snipe

Tail feathers of painted snipe

White stork

Bill clattering of the white stork (left) is the typical sound communication used between storks, especially when the sexes greet each other on the nest. The outer tail feathers of snipe (far left) are much stiffer than the central ones and are held together with tiny hooks. When the male snipe dives at an angle of 45° the tail feathers vibrate with a drumming or beating sound. The tail of the pintail snipe have extra stiffened outer tail feathers.

parents' sounds, it will produce a song which has the same basic pattern and sequence as an adult's song, but which lacks the more difficult – and often more musical – parts. The full song is gradually built onto the basic pattern only after hearing the parents sing during the summer months. One experiment involving nightingales showed that in order to learn the complete song, a young bird had to see as well as hear the parent bird.

The amount of time taken to learn songs varies from species to species. Birds from temperate regions (where territoriality is strong) learn their songs at an early age, whereas in tropical regions (with less territoriality) the learning of song patterns goes on for a longer period of time.

Mimicry
There are some species where the majority of the song appears to be innate. Song sparrows, for instance, do not need to hear a parent or any other song sparrow to develop a perfect song pattern. When they do hear one, however, they develop a song which mimics the bird they hear. As a result, song sparrows may have as many

as 900 distinct local dialects.

As well as learning their own songs, many birds are excellent mimics, building the phrases of other species into their own songs. The Indian hill mynah is an accomplished mimic in captivity, to the extent that it can even copy human speech; in the wild, however, it does not incorporate the songs of other birds into its own. On the other hand, there is the marsh warbler, which breeds in Europe and winters in Africa, whose song is made up almost entirely of phrases from other species. Studies have shown that these consist of a mixture of phrases from nearly 100 European species and over 100 African species. Each individual bird can mimic about 75 species; the most common European bird phrases come from blackbird, house and tree sparrows, whitethroat, and swallow, while the commonest African species are common bulbul, green-backed camaroptera, black-backed puffback, tawny-flanked prinia, and red-faced cisticola. The most notable North American mimic is the mockingbird, known to imitate 55 species in an hour. Catbirds and yellow-breasted chats are also good mimics.

WHEN BIRDS SING

IN TEMPERATE REGIONS, the amount of daylight plays an important part in the life of all birds. It tells migrants when to migrate, and it also triggers the production of hormones which prepare birds for the breeding season. Singing is stimulated by the presence of the male sex hormone, testosterone, produced when daylight length reaches a certain amount – usually in excess of 12 hours. In temperate regions, this results in a distinct breeding season during which the majority of birds breed. In the tropics, where the change in day length is minimal, other factors may also be responsible, which is why breeding occurs throughout the year in such areas. As bird song is linked so closely to breeding, most singing takes place during the breeding season.

The length of song period varies from species to species, and the timing of the breeding season differs geographically. Birds which breed in temperate regions have a clearly defined breeding season. Many birds begin singing in earnest at the beginning of the year, so as to establish their territories early on. As spring approaches more and more birds sing, and with the arrival of spring migrants the chorus is complete. In the northern hemisphere there is nothing to compare with the woodland dawn chorus in early May.

For the most part, spring visitors will have been silent on their wintering grounds, but as they prepare to migrate they often begin to sing. The song is often

Red-backed shrike

A male indigo bunting (above) chooses a prominent perch to sing from. It is a summer visitor to North America and sings throughout the day from May well into August, later than many other songbirds.

Redstart

Lyre bird

Side view of Lyre bird

Lesser superb bird of paradise

very tentative to start with, and far from perfect; many young birds will be singing for the first time. When these migrants eventually reach their breeding grounds they will be in full song, ready to establish a territory and find a mate.

PROMPTED BY DAYLIGHT

LENGTHENING DAYLIGHT HOURS encourage resident birds to sing; as the days get longer their singing becomes more pronounced and continues for longer periods. Wintering birds are often silent for the whole of their stay, but occasionally some of the late-leavers may be stimulated into song by a particularly spring-like day. Birds can be fooled by light levels, and some will begin to sing in the fall when the daylight length matches that of spring. This singing soons stops as the days get shorter, however.

In most species, song is at its fullest at the start of breeding, with males singing throughout the day. It wanes slightly during courtship and mating, and picks up again during the incubation period, although males which help with the incubation will sing less. As soon as the eggs hatch and help is needed to feed the young, the male will sing less often, concentrating his territorial song on the area around the nest.

Many birds go silent and molt when their young fledge and need no more supervision. Others may have a second brood; if so, the male will sing again with renewed ardor, often re-establishing territorial boundaries. In the late summer or fall the hormonal drive tails off, and many birds stop singing altogether, though this pattern of song is a generalization and there are some species which do not conform. The mockingbird and cardinal, for instance, sing in every season as they defend their territories throughout the year, while the brown thrasher ceases singing immediately after mating.

As well as this annual variation in song, there is also a daily rhythm. Birds which are active during the day will begin singing before sunrise as the increasing light reaches a certain intensity. As the morning progresses, birds begin to quiet down; singing picks up in the late afternoon, continuing until nearly dusk.

Different species are triggered into song by varying amounts of light, and when listening to a dawn chorus separate species can be noted as they start. The order in which birds first sing is fairly constant, though it depends upon the birds present. If they are in the vicinity, robins are usually the first to pipe up. In eastern states, the next to sing might be a wood thrush and then a Carolina wren, while out West it would most likely be a hermit thrush and then a Bewick's wren. Chickadees, phoebes, towhees, and sparrows are also early risers.

The Eastern phoebe (above) is a North American bird common around gardens and farms.

The red-eyed vireo (left) has the distinction of being the most vociferous of songsters.

A red-winged blackbird (above) sings silhouetted against the moon.

The yellow-breasted chat (below) is another North American bird that may sing its long bugling notes well into the night.

It is interesting to note that thrushes are commonly found to be the first singers in most countries. In Europe, the blackbird is often first, followed by the song thrush. In India one of the first is the Indian robin; in southern Africa it is the kurrichane and olive thrushes. In New Zealand, with its high number of introduced European birds, it is once again the blackbird and song thrush which begin the chorus.

The contrast between the dawn chorus and the quiet of midday is truly astonishing when you realize the birds are still wide awake, though once again there are exceptions, as certain birds sing consistently throughout the day. Field sparrows, indigo buntings, red-eyed vireos, and prairie warblers are just a few examples. Actually, the red-eyed vireo holds the world record for the number of songs given in a day – a total of 22,197!

Nighttime vocalists

Night is not solely reserved for owls – it is often surprising just what else can be heard under the cover of darkness on a spring night. Mockingbirds are the North American equivalent of the legendary nightingale and can be heard regularly at night, together with yellow-breasted chats. Outbursts of "ecstasy" singing from yellowthroats and ovenbirds add to the night chorus which, of course, also includes woodcocks, and whip-poor-wills.

WHERE BIRDS SING

An exposed song perch allows songs to be heard more easily, reaching the ears of both rivals and potential mates. In an urban area with few natural song posts this European blackbird (above) has found a suitable alternative perch from which to broadcast its message.

Birds of more open habitat often have a distinctive song flight. The tree pipit (left) will fly from a perch high into the air and then deliver its song while floating down to the ground with wings outstretched in what is called its "parachute" display flight.

AS THE MAIN PURPOSE of song is to attract a mate and deter competitors, it follows that the further a song carries the better. For this reason many male singers will choose a prominent perch, such as the top of a tall tree, bush, or rock, and sometimes an artificial song post at the top of a telephone pole or tall building. The song post may be positioned at the edge of a territory, whose boundaries are often marked by a number of song posts. The actual nest is normally sited well within the territory and, especially with large territories, the male will sing from a perch well away from the nest so as not to attract predators directly to it.

For bird watchers, the fact that different singing birds choose different but consistent perching places helps to locate the bird. This is particularly true of many woodland species, especially warblers. When spring migration is in full swing, a piece of woodland can contain dozens of different species and it helps enormously that black-throated blue warblers sing from the undergrowth, black-throated green warblers from a middle height, and Cape May warblers from the very top. These levels are also the birds' usual feeding points, so they can be looked for with a greater chance of success even when silent. However, singing, feeding, and nesting levels are not always the same; many thrushes which feed on the ground, for instance, will nest off the ground and sing from the top of a tree. Also, in open areas such as fields, prairie, tundra, and desert, many birds deliver their songs during flight. Larks, longspurs and pipits will "perch" in the air to deliver their songs.

Birds which sing from exposed perches tend to have shorter song phrases, possibly to reduce the chance of a predator catching them unawares in mid-song. Certainly some of the longest songs come from species which stay well hidden, such as the grasshopper warbler, which has a trilling song lasting for more than two minutes. The possible extra vulnerability means that normally song perches are positioned where the singer can see a predator coming, and also near to cover for escape. When birds are establishing song posts, they often try out a few, eventually settling for the safest one which lets them communicate to the widest audience.

The nightingale (above) is a bird which breeds in dense woodland and thicket. To make its presence known it has a loud and beautiful song. To increase its chance of contacting a mate the male habitually sings at night when little else is making a sound.

Weed stalks may provide a song post for a bright spring-plumaged bobolink (below), but he also has a fluttering song flight. Summer visitors to North America, the males arrive back several days before the females and fill the air with their tinkling song.

IDENTIFYING SONGBIRDS

TO THE INEXPERIENCED bird watcher, the way in which a practiced ear can pick out and identify bird sounds seems almost supernatural. Most beginners cannot imagine ever mastering the different sounds, but with practice it becomes relatively easy. Most people aware of birds will recognize the songs of many birds around them: mockingbirds, robins, chickadees, jays, titmice, and cardinals are some more familiar species and families. Learning to recognize the commoner species provides a basis from which to expand. Having learned the songs and calls of birds in your backyard, say, visit a woodland where many of these familiar birds will be present. Listen for the sounds you know and pick out any unfamiliar ones. Try and track down and identify the singer, remembering that where a bird sings from will often help with its identification. Also, try to compare any unknown songs with a familiar one as this may often be a clue to the family of the bird you are hearing. Whenever possible, go out

with a more experienced bird watcher who will be able to draw your attention to the similarities and differences of songs, and also pick out and emphasize the important phrases.

An additional help may be a recording of bird song, either on record or cassette. There are a wide variety to choose from – some will play all species in systematic order, others may select the commoner species, and still others present birds found in a particular habitat. All are a great help to the bird watcher who wants to become familiar with the bewildering number of sounds that birds make. The great advantage of recordings, of course, is that they can be played again and again, thereby providing you with the ideal opportunity to familiarize yourself with the bird | songs.

Translating bird song
Some bird songs are easier to remember than others since they lend themselves to verbal descriptions.

Bird watchers on the reed-fringed shore of Lake McIlwaine, Zimbabwe (left).

A bird watcher using citizen band radio updates a rare bird sighting. News spreads fast among the ornithological fraternity and rare sightings bring enthusiasts out from far afield to what could be a once in a life-time chance to glimpse an unusual bird (below).

Whip-poor-wills actually say *whip-poor-will*, and the song of the ovenbird can be clearly written as *teacher-teacher-teacher*. Unfortunately, such descriptions cannot be found to fit all songs and calls. For example, one guide describes the robin as having a "loud, liquid song, a variable *cheerily cheer-up cheerio*," which gives a very good idea of the quality and rhythm of the sound but doesn't really help if you've never heard the sound of a robin before.

If you don't have a tape recorder, it is useful to familiarize yourself with a means of writing down songs and calls, as this may help to identify them later. Early attempts made use of musical notation, and while this is versatile enough to describe the notes, speed, pitch, and duration of a song, there are few people with the ability to apply it accurately or to interpret it afterwards. Written descriptions are possibly the best way of all, though again what you hear and write down may not correspond with what is written in a book. The most difficult parts to transcribe are often the consonant sounds, as it is usually the vowel sounds which contain the character of the song. And don't forget that as well as the sound, some idea of the length of each note or syllable is needed. Add to this an indication of whether successive notes are higher or lower, or if a note is rising or falling, and quite a complicated system is required. One method uses a line above the written sounds to indicate length, rise, or fall in pitch, and

Bird watching in the Florida Everglades (left).

Bird watchers using binoculars and telescopes on a beach maximize sightings of off-shore sea birds (above).

perhaps sound quality, such as a trill. Capital letters can be used to differentiate soft and loud notes. No system is foolproof, however, and it is worth practicing by writing out songs from a recording and comparing it with the description in a book.

RECORDING BIRD SONG

MANY BIRD WATCHERS also become bird photographers, sometimes simply to record a particular sighting as a memento, but often in an attempt to get better and better pictures which might possibly be published. Similarly, many bird enthusiasts take up bird sound recording.

To get the best results, specialized and often expensive equipment is needed. With present-day technology, the large reel-to-reel tape recorders of the past have all but vanished, and nowadays portable cassette recorders and light, hand-held microphones can produce high-quality recordings. If you buy cheaply the results are likely to be poor, so it's always worth investing in quality equipment. The recorder's microphone is its most important feature, and it may be necessary to have a feature for eliminating background noise, especially in woodland, where other birds may be singing at the same time. There is such a wide choice of microphones and a bewildering number of terms to contend with – do you want a condenser or dynamic type? omni- or uni-directional? with or without parabolic reflector? – that the best way to choose is to seek advice first from a bird watcher who already records sounds.

The same applies to the type of recorder. Cassette recorders are the cheapest, and there are many to choose from. Reel-to-reel recorders are more expensive, but they allow you to edit tapes by cutting and splicing, and also to slow down recordings to analyze the sound. If you simply want to listen to what you have recorded, cassettes are your best bet. Remember that the frequency response is one of the most important features of a recorder, and if you want to faithfully record the high trills of warblers the response should go up to more than 10,000 Hertz. Just as important, however, is that the equipment will stand up to the rigors of life in the field, so it must be both durable and waterproof. Be warned that bird sound recording can be addictive; many a bird watcher has all but forsaken his binoculars for a microphone and recorder.

The recording of bird sounds has had one major effect on ornithology – the invention of the sound spectrogram or sonogram, a method of recording bird

Out in the field an ornithologist up early to record winter migrants (above). The aluminium reflector for channelling the sound is painted green for camouflage. It is linked to a professional reel-to-reel tape recorder. Headphones are used to monitor the recording.

Unobtrusive dress and movements are key to success in getting close to birds. After stalking a warbler in camouflaged clothing, a bird watcher focuses on an early spring migrant (right).

sounds visually as a graphical representation showing pitch and frequency. Sonograms tend to look like a series of smudges, and are reproduced in some field guides and handbooks. These can be interpreted with practice, though are not of much use in the field.

ATTRACTING BIRDS

THE FRUSTRATIONS OF BIRD-WATCHING in dense woodland – where birds can be heard but not seen – can often be great. However, birds' sounds and their reaction to certain sounds can be used to a bird watcher's advantage.

From the bird enthusiast's point of view, one of the most useful types of bird behavior is that of mobbing. By imitating the call of an owl, or better still using a tape recording, birds can be drawn in by their instinctive

mobbing reaction. Imitating alarm calls can also work in this way, as does "pishing" and squeaking. These last two terms describe noises easily made by any bird watcher. The first is made simply by pursing your lips and blowing out, and, if repeated rapidly, will usually attract warblers, flycatchers, thrushes, and a whole host of other birds. A squeaking sound is made by kissing the back of your hand. Practice will soon show which noise gives the best response. Owl imitations are less easy and potentially harmful, as well, since the persistent use of an imitation or recording of an owl's call could lead to a bird abandoning its territory. Even more likely to cause disruption in the breeding season is the use of a bird's own song to trick it into thinking there is a rival male in its territory. Birds respond so vigorously to this ploy they have even been known to attack the offending tape recorder in their frenzy to drive off the intruder. Some nature reserves now ban

A pair of nightingales attack a stuffed cuckoo (above). It was found that the cuckoo's head caused the strongest aggressive response in the nightingales.

A party of ornithologists (below) make their way through the Amazon Forest. In such closed habitats bird song features strongly as a means of communication between species.

the use of tape recorders because of their effects on birds when used by a steady stream of bird watchers. Careful and limited use of these techniques, however, should aid the birder without disturbing the birds.

OUT IN THE FIELD

FAMILIARITY WITH SONGBIRDS is gained by many hours afield; hearing unfamiliar calls, tracking them down and then studying the individual as it sings. As this is being done many other fragments that will lead to birding competence are being collected. You will begin to understand habitat preference, activity hours for a specific species, preferred levels of activity within the forest for feeding and singing, time of the year when the bird is most active and perhaps information on the bird's food preference.

The barest of essentials are binoculars and a good field guide. On the market today there is an overwhelming selection of binoculars. Which one you end up with is often dictated by your pocketbook but a few things should be considered. Prices may range from

$35 to nearly $1000! How can there be such a wide differentiation? As might be expected quality is a main factor.

The very expensive models are optically perfect for viewing under a wide range of conditions from very low light to looking directly toward a lighted subject. Grinding of the glass allows for maximum use of light under all conditions. They are usually waterproof and dustproof. Nothing can be more frustrating than having binoculars fog in a moist situation and prevent you from birding. The prisms of the expensive models are anchored in place much better and this prevents slippage in heat or when jarred and thereby prevents knocking the binoculars out of alignment. When you pay a lower price many of these features are lost. In addition the more expensive glasses are either designed or can be modified to focus extremely close, a feature that is a must for tropical or dense thicket birding.

However, for $150 or so a good pair of binoculars can be had that will fit the average birder's needs. As for power, ask three people and you might get three answers. The standard, and a good choice, is 7 × 35 with center and right eye focus. The seven power will allow a very wide depth of field and therefore one need

The excitement of the hunt gathers momentum (right) as a dozen "twitchers" or more focus on a rare North American migrant blown far west out of its usual range onto the Isles of Scilly.

Well prepared for a winter's day bird watching, a birder (left) focuses his scope on wading birds out on the mud flats.

not keep focusing and re-focusing. In the open spaces of the West, 10 power can certainly be useful when viewing over such great distances but in the "up close" birding of the eastern forest, 10 power can be very difficult to use. In addition, the higher the power the more likely that the vibration while holding the binoculars will distort the view. Do not be fooled into "the more power, the better I'll see the bird" syndrome. People afield with 15 and 20 power binoculars will find them worthless. If you do a lot of low light birding then 7 × 50 might be better to allow more light in under low level conditions. Take the time and look through the binoculars you will purchase; they need to be right to make birding fully enjoyable.

Scopes

While we are on optics, the question of which scope is best arises. Again, there are many scopes on the market today. Most run in the $200 plus bracket. Here, too, it is important to look through the scope before you purchase it if you can. Some scopes impart a greenish tint, some a bluish, some neutral. Different eyes view colors differently, and you need to get one that pleases your eye. Also, do not be fooled by the "zoom to great power" feature. Once past 35 power it takes exceptional light conditions or one of the amazing $3000 level scopes to make the high power worth it. In most scopes the field of view becomes narrow and the image blurred. The ideal scope power is with an eyepiece of $20\times$, $25\times$ or $30\times$. You can stay with one power and have as backup a $30\times$ if needed, then just switch eyepieces. Most of the time, $20\times$ can handle all needs. In addition, when choosing a tripod be sure it is light and quick to set up. Some tripods have more levers and handles on them than the cockpit of a 747. Stay away from these! What they do is prevent you from wanting to use the scope. Birders may jump out of their cars, set up their scopes and finish scoping an area by the time a multi-handled tripod is just coming into place. It's back into the car and the complex job never did get set up. So go with light and simple. If it's the right one, the scope and tripod will become a part of you afield and you will carry it everywhere with no encumbrance.

BACKYARD BIRD-WATCHING

FOR THOSE PEOPLE WHO ENJOY the natural world around them, the presence of birds in their own backyard or garden can only bring pleasure. Enthusiasts lucky enough to have large gardens can entice a wide variety of species by providing the right environment, and even small yards can be made attractive to birds. Many bird watchers get as much enjoyment out of a new visitor to their backyard as they do from sighting the rarest of vagrants.

For a yard to be attractive to birds, it must provide sufficient food, breeding sites, and protection. The most successful ones will reproduce something of the birds' natural habitat, especially those in which some parts have been left in a wild state to provide seeds and berries for food, and thick cover for nesting and roosting. It should also be left untreated by pesticides in order that a full community of insects and invertebrates can also live there and provide further food. Such an area should have something to attract both breeding birds and winter visitors, ensuring a variety of birds throughout the year.

The European robin (left) is one species which has adapted from a woodland to a garden habitat. Often tame and confiding, its bright color, cheeky nature and sweet song make it a welcome visitor.

One of North America's larger backyard birds is the blue jay (above). Although omnivorous it eats mostly nuts and seeds. Oak and beech trees will provide it with food which it may carry off to store.

PLANTING FOR SUCCESS

THE MOST ATTRACTIVELY MANAGED gardens for birds will contain: food plants, which can be a mixture of native and ornamental types; trees and shrubs, to provide further food, shelter, nesting sites, song posts, and protection from predators; nest boxes, to provide suitable sites which do not occur naturally; a source of water, both for drinking and bathing (either a pond or a simple birdbath); and a winter feeding station, to provide a variety of foods (and which is visible from a watch point).

The food plants, trees, and shrubs that are best for a bird garden will depend on what region of the country the garden is in, as well as its size. Native trees providing both cover and food are ideal. Red Oaks provide nesting places and cover, and produce acorns; they grow best in the East. Beech produces a nut which is eaten by blackbirds and blue jays; ash has a winged seed eaten by purple finches and grosbeaks; and mountain ash berries attract waxwings, robins and

A young cardinal (left) perches on a spicebush. Berry-bearing bushes will help to attract birds into any garden. Some of the best are mountain ash, holly, elderberry, hawthorn, and honeysuckle.

Many flowers produce seeds for birds. The Eurasian goldfinch (below) is one of the species which likes thistle seeds. Sunflowers produce seeds which are popular with titmice, nuthatches, and finches.

orioles. Fruits from various types of cherry are eaten by more than 80 species. Evergreens provide some of the best protection, while red cedars or junipers also provide berries, and white pine forms cones which hold seeds for siskins, nuthatches, and many other species. Berry-bearing bushes and shrubs are also essential – roses, hawthorns, holly, buckthorn, and elderberry are some of the best. Of the non-native shrubs, cotoneaster produces a prolific harvest of berries and comes in a wide variety of cultivated forms. Climbing plants such as ivy, honeysuckle, and Virginia creeper are useful in smaller yards, where they can grow up a wall to provide nesting and roosting places, as well as berries.

Birds which prefer low scrub and bushes can be enticed into a garden if a brush pile is made: a thick tangle of pruned branches and swept leaves should be left in a corner where birds can hide themselves. The shyer catbirds, thrashers, towhees, and thrushes especially like these arrangements. Also, in winter, the branches can harbor invertebrates for wrens and other insect-feeders to find.

Many attractive flowers produce seeds for winter finches. Sunflower heads can be left on the plant, or collected and put out at a feeding station. Their seeds are great favorites of all birds, and are eaten by

Climbing shrubs provide nesting habitat when grown against walls. The guelder rose (above) is a good example and it also attracts insects to its flowers as well as producing large red hips.

Thick conifers and evergreens (left) protect nests well and are very useful for roosting birds in the winter. Some produce seeds which are a good source of energy.

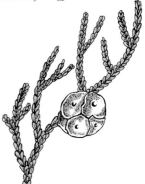

A popular ornamental shrub is the cotoneaster (below). All varieties produce clusters of red berries.

The oak (above) probably feeds and houses more birds than any other tree. Insects for warblers, acorns for jays, and mature trees contain nest holes for nuthatches.

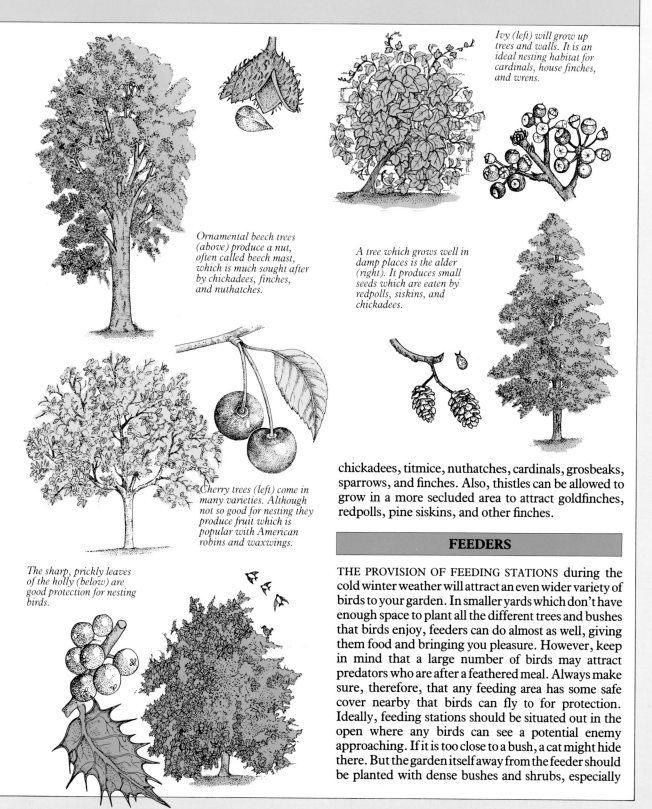

Ivy (left) will grow up trees and walls. It is an ideal nesting habitat for cardinals, house finches, and wrens.

Ornamental beech trees (above) produce a nut, often called beech mast, which is much sought after by chickadees, finches, and nuthatches.

A tree which grows well in damp places is the alder (right). It produces small seeds which are eaten by redpolls, siskins, and chickadees.

Cherry trees (left) come in many varieties. Although not so good for nesting they produce fruit which is popular with American robins and waxwings.

The sharp, prickly leaves of the holly (below) are good protection for nesting birds.

chickadees, titmice, nuthatches, cardinals, grosbeaks, sparrows, and finches. Also, thistles can be allowed to grow in a more secluded area to attract goldfinches, redpolls, pine siskins, and other finches.

FEEDERS

THE PROVISION OF FEEDING STATIONS during the cold winter weather will attract an even wider variety of birds to your garden. In smaller yards which don't have enough space to plant all the different trees and bushes that birds enjoy, feeders can do almost as well, giving them food and bringing you pleasure. However, keep in mind that a large number of birds may attract predators who are after a feathered meal. Always make sure, therefore, that any feeding area has some safe cover nearby that birds can fly to for protection. Ideally, feeding stations should be situated out in the open where any birds can see a potential enemy approaching. If it is too close to a bush, a cat might hide there. But the garden itself away from the feeder should be planted with dense bushes and shrubs, especially evergreens, which provide protection from avian predators such as hawks.

Many birds forage over a large area for their food, and even birds that visit feeders may go to several gardens in turn. As a result, it is difficult to judge how many birds actually make use of the garden. You may see no more than a dozen chickadees at a time, but there could be more than 50 visiting each day. Their foraging instinct may be such that they tend not to feed in one place for long before moving on. Then again, some species, like evening grosbeaks and house finches, will feed as long as there is food; they will rest near the feeders when the food is finished and feed again when more is put out.

A simple food platform – a wooden tray fixed onto a post, window sill, or tree stump – will bring many birds right up to your window. A roof is not essential, but it does serve to keep food dry. Feeders can be hung from the platform or from tree branches, and these can be used to dispense seeds, nuts, and other food.

Ultimately, the key to a successful feeding station is to place out as wide a variety of foods as possible. Seed mixtures contain different-sized seeds for different birds, for instance, millet, thistle, hemp, sunflower, corn, and wheat. Peanuts and peanut butter are very popular – the latter can be smeared onto branches or placed out in log feeders. Fatty foods like suet provide birds with the most energy. It can be placed out in lumps, or melted and mixed with seeds to form a cake. Scraps of food such as cheese, meat fat, and bones will also be gratefully received. Fruit is a favorite of many

A seed hopper (above) will gradually dispense seed into the tray and allow many days' *supply to be put out at one time. It is especially useful if someone is going away.*

A globe feeder (above) stores a supply of seed and keeps it dry.

Instead of buying an expensive feeder, try using a suspended jar (above) which keeps the food dry and attracts titmice.

An empty coconut shell (above) can be filled with a "birdcake," made from melted fat and seeds, which has set before hanging.

A tree stump (above) can be used as a feeding station by boring a hole in it and filling it with fat, seeds, fruit, and nuts.

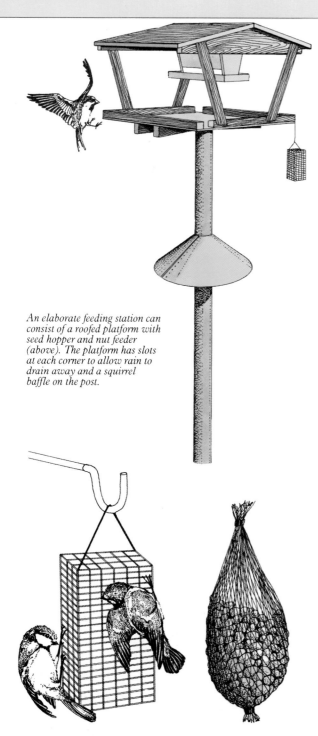

An elaborate feeding station can consist of a roofed platform with seed hopper and nut feeder (above). The platform has slots at each corner to allow rain to drain away and a squirrel baffle on the post.

birds – apples, raisins, cherries, oranges, and figs will all be eaten, and are excellent as summer food.

Bird feeders are used most after the breeding season, in the fall around October through the winter until early spring. Remember that while food attracts birds to where you can see them, it is only in severe winters that feeding may be vital. Also, feeding throughout the year is not always beneficial for birds. Many will leave the feeders as soon as natural foods become available again in spring, but some will continue to use them if food is present. Birds change their diets as the natural food sources change; those which feed on nothing but nuts and seeds in the winter will be eating insects and grubs in the summer. The young of these birds need soft insect food when they are developing, however, and if the parents give them unnatural foods from a feeder it can cause harm. Young birds may be unable to digest it properly, and it might not contain all the necessary nutrition for their normal growth.

One group of birds which can be readily fed in the summer are the hummingbirds. Although not songbirds, they still make an attractive addition to the garden, as do the flowers they feed on, such as trumpet vine, fuchsia, gladiolus, columbine, nasturtium, petunia, hollyhock, and morning glory. Artificial feeders with a sugary solution inside can also be used, but care must be taken to make up the solution correctly and to change it regularly. One part sugar mixed with four parts water, followed by boiling, produces a good energy-rich food. It must be stored in a refrigerator, and feeders should be cleaned before refilling.

A simple wire cage (above) can be used for nuts and other scraps. Only agile birds can cling on to feed.

A mesh bag filled with peanuts (above) attracts finches. Hanging it from a long string stops larger birds from feeding.

Peanuts in their shells (above) can be threaded and hung out. It is fun to watch chickadees open the shells to get at the nuts.

A small log (above) can be drilled with holes and stuffed with suet and nuts. Woodpeckers will feed from it.

With large numbers of birds feeding, a considerable amount of droppings will accumulate around the feeding stations, which should be moved occasionally to avoid contaminatiing the food of ground-feeding birds. In addition, the accumulation of droppings can facilitate the passing on of diseases from one bird to another. If the feeding stations can't easily be moved, it's best to disinfect the ground occasionally.

Cats and squirrels can be a great nuisance in a good bird garden. The former scare away the birds and occasionally catch them, while the latter will steal food from feeding stations and may also attack nest boxes. Feeding stations and nestboxes on posts can be protected by using a baffle halfway up the post. Barbed wire is unsightly but often effective, as well, although thorny cuttings from roses, holly, or hawthorn, tied in a bundle, works just as well. A bell-collar on a cat may give the birds warning of its presence and prevent them being caught. If a cat has a favorite position on a fence or under a bush, some prickly cuttings placed there will soon convince it to move on.

Some birds store the food they find. Nuthatches, titmice, and jays, in particular, will frequently take seeds, nuts, and suet which they then hide in a crevice or in the ground. They will return later for it – if it has not been stolen by other opportunist birds or squirrels which have seen them hide it!

It is debatable whether putting food out for birds during winter actually helps them to survive, except in the severest conditions. During a mild winter, the supply of natural food available will often keep birds away from feeders, especially if the trees have pro-duced a good nut crop. The time when birds most need food is when the temperatures are low and snow covers their normal food sources. Food is all-important to birds as it provides the energy they need to survive. At night they lose energy in the form of heat, and during the day they lose more in the search for food. If they can't find enough food to replace the energy they have lost they will eventually die. It is not just the provision of food that helps but also the fact that it is easily found and is there when needed. Food should always be placed out regularly during the winter months so that the birds can anticipate it and, if need be, rely upon it.

A good bird garden will also provide roosting places for birds so they don't need to travel far in order to feed when the weather is at its coldest. Sparrows, grosbeaks, and finches will simply perch deep within an evergreen, sheltered from the wind, rain, or snow. A yellow-rumped warbler has even been known to roost each night on a Christmas tree in someone's house. Some birds will make use of a vacant nestbox; there is one case recorded of 31 winter wrens using the same box.

As well as simply looking at or listening to the birds in your backyard, it can be interesting to study their behavior, especially when feeding. Many exhibit a pecking order either within their own species or between different species. Among birds of the same species, males will often dominate females and not let them feed at the same time, while young birds may be driven off by older ones. There are always some species which appear more aggressive than others, displacing the more timid ones from the feeders. Occasionally a

Beware — the versatile gray squirrel will raid even the most well-positioned bird feeder (right).

FEEDING AND NESTING REQUIREMENTS

Measurements of nestboxes are given as width×depth×height; nest hole dimensions refer to the diameter of the nest hole.

SPECIES	FOOD/FEEDING	NESTING/NESTBOX
GREAT-CRESTED FLYCATCHER	Insects and fruit. Feeds among mature trees in orchards	Nests naturally in tree holes. Box 6×6×10in with 2in nest hole, placed above 6ft.
TREE SWALLOW	Insects caught over ponds and rivers; bayberries in fall.	Uses natural tree holes. Box 5×5×6in with 1½in hole, placed high on tree or under eaves of old building.
BLUE JAY	Omnivorous, especially nuts and fruit, takes sunflower seeds, peanuts and suet at feeder.	Nest of twigs placed 10-15ft high in trees, bushes, vines. Oak and beech trees provide both food and nest sites.
BLACK-CAPPED CHICKADEE	Insects, seeds and fruit; takes peanuts, cornmeal and sunflower seeds from feeder.	Usually excavates hole in rotten branch. Box 4×4×8in with 1⅛in hole, placed above 8ft.
TUFTED PLAIN TITMOUSE	Seeds, nuts and fruit; takes sunflower seeds, suet and peanuts at feeder.	Natural cavities. Box 4×4×8in with 1¼in hole placed above 8ft.
HOUSE/BEWICK'S WREN	Insects and spiders. Will take finely ground suet and nuts from ground.	Nests in almost any cavity. Box 4×4×8in with 1in hole at 5 to 10ft.
EASTERN/WESTERN BLUEBIRD	Insects and fruit; at feeder likes peanut butter, cornmeal and mealworms.	Natural tree holes. Box 5×5×8in with 1½in hole placed at 5 to 10ft.
ROBIN	Worms, insects and fruit; cakes, bread, raisins and apples at feeder. Likes most berry bushes.	Nests on tree forks, in bushes and will use ledges and shelves.
NORTHERN MOCKINGBIRD	Insects and fruit; takes suet and raisins at feeder. Likes fruits of elderberry, blackberry and red cedar.	Nests in bush, vine or tree such as red cedar or pine.
BROWN THRASHER	Insects and berries, sometimes nuts and corn; will take suet, wheat, millet and sunflower seeds from feeder.	Nests in low bushes such as white currant, lilac, privet, plum, and in brush piles.
CEDAR WAXWING	Fruit and insects; at feeder will take raisins, currants and apples. Particularly fond of berries from mountain ash, pyracantha, privet, cedar and mulberries.	Nests in trees and shrubs where food is plentiful.
NORTHERN CARDINAL	Insects, fruit and seeds, especially of pine; comes to feeder for cracked wheat and sunflower seeds.	Nests in trees, thickets and vines. In garden likes young evergreens, rosebushes and and honeysuckle.
SONG SPARROW	Insects, seeds and fruit; comes for seed mixtures placed on ground.	Nests in long grass and low bushes.
WHITE-CROWNED SPARROW	Seeds and insects. Comes to feeder for millet and seed mixtures.	Nests on ground, in grass or under shrubs, sometimes in small conifer.
DARK-EYED JUNCO	Insects and seeds; takes seed mixtures at feeder, also attracted by seeds of zinnias and cosmos.	Nests on ground under tree roots, in brush piles and under house gables.
HOUSE FINCH	Seeds, fruit and insects; takes mixed seeds, fruit and scraps from feeders.	Nests in holes in trees and buildings. Box 6×6×6in with 2in hole placed at 8 to 12ft.
PURPLE FINCH	Seeds, insects and fruit; visits feeder for hemp, millet and sunflower seeds.	Nests high in dense conifers and deciduous trees.
NORTHERN ORIOLE	Insects and fruit. Comes to feeder for apple, orange, banana, grapes and suet.	Suspends nest from branch of maple, elm, poplar or conifer.
SCARLET TANAGER	Insects and berries; comes to feeder for peanut butter, cornmeal, apple, banana, cherries and raisins.	Nests on branch of large oak, ash or maple.

Birds can be encouraged to breed in gardens by providing a suitable nest site. This spotted flycatcher (right) is using a shelf which has been carefully placed against a wall behind a climbing rose.

bird may make a feeder, or even a berry bush, its own – robins sometimes do this – and will drive off all intruders. If you notice that some birds are monopolizing a feeding station, try to spread out the food so that others can get to it. Don't just put seed in feeders or on a platform – throw some on the ground, as well, broadcasting it rather than placing it in one small area.

During winter months, water is as important to

A good bird garden should provide water as well as food. Regular baths (above) keep this mistle thrush's plumage clean and waterproof.

birds as food. They not only need to drink water, but must have it to bathe in, as well. Birds' feathers are very important as insulation, and to perform efficiently must be clean and dry. The air trapped underneath the feathers helps to insulate, which is why birds fluff out their feathers in cold weather. Regular bathing and preening enables them to clean and waterproof their feathers with natural oils. A supply of clean water should be available at all times and should be kept ice-free. Water is also equally important throughout the summer, when fresh water may be difficult to find. A simple birdbath will suffice for most birds, but a small pond with suitable vegetation near it will often attract birds that are otherwise difficult to spot in the wild. Never make a pond too deep, and be sure there are shallow edges. Branches laid into the water will provide perches.

AN ASSORTMENT OF NEST BOXES

WHILE A GARDEN CAN PROVIDE relatively natural nest sites for birds which build in bushes, trees, and grass, those birds who nest in tree holes rarely find a natural site. This is where bird boxes are indispensable. Boxes can be made to suit a wide range of species, and should always be positioned in appropriate locations. When constructing a box, it is important to get the hole size correct for the species you want to attract. The box should have the right internal dimensions, as well – not

A European robin (left) carries nesting material to its nest, which may be in a nestbox, on the shelf of a shed or even in an old kettle. A good nest site is protected from both predators and weather.

A nestbox should never be placed facing into the prevailing wind. If the box is tilted slightly downwards (below) this will reduce the risk of rain getting in and chilling the nestlings.

A nestbox (above) is rarely too deep as the bird will fill the space with nesting material to its preferred height. Too shallow a box might allow a predator to reach in and take the young.

too big or too small. Lastly, the hole should not be too close to the floor nor too high up, although some birds may fill the box with nesting material until a suitable height is reached. Once built, the box must be positioned correctly as some birds will nest higher than others. Most boxes are simply fixed securely to a tree trunk, though purple martins like their boxes on a post. Bluebirds, wrens, chickadees, titmice, nuthatches, and swallows will all use boxes, while barn swallows, phoebes, and robins prefer shelf nests (simply boxes with no fronts and sometimes no sides). Remember that birds are territorial when breeding, and if you fill a garden with dozens of boxes it is likely that only a few will be used.

Boxes should be cleaned out and repaired at the end of the nesting season. Removing an old nest will often remove parasites and their eggs which are lying dormant until the next breeding season, waiting to infest the young. If nestboxes are left up outside the breeding season some birds such as wrens, titmice, chickadees, nuthatches, and bluebirds may roost in them.

Gardens which attract songbirds will always be full of activity throughout the year. Pleasure can be derived from watching the birds feed in winter, seeing them courting or squabbling over territories in the spring and raising their young in the summer. The arrival of the first migrants in spring and fall can be most exciting and the occasional rare visitor will always be rewarding. A bird garden need not be untidy and overgrown and will contain more life than any carefully manicured, weed and pest free example of the horticulturalist's art.

A hole-fronted box (above) is good for house finches, chickadees, wrens, and titmice.

An open-fronted box (above) will appeal to some flycatchers. It should be partly hidden in foliage to keep away predators.

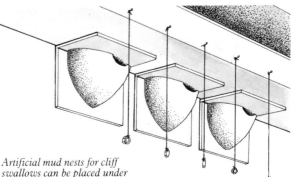

Artificial mud nests for cliff swallows can be placed under the eaves (above). Weighted strings will stop house sparrows from moving in.

Sometimes the urge to feed young can be too great. This blue tit (above) has been attracted by the calls of baby wrens and is busy feeding them instead of its own brood.

Lengths of doweling are used for perches inside the roosting box so that many birds can enter (above).

Some birds will use nestboxes as winter roosts. A roosting box can be made with an entrance hole and perch (above).

Each layer of the martin house must be removable to allow easy cleaning. The roof contains ventilation holes (above).

Each floor contains eight accessible compartments. The central compartment allows air to circulate through the house (above).

Purple martins are colonial nesters and prefer an apartment block to a single nestbox (above). Their high-rise accommodation is about 20 ft from the ground and must be lowered for cleaning each year.

Brown creepers normally nest in a narrow tree crevice. A strip of bark fixed to a tree may be used for nesting or roosting (above).

A more formal creeper box can be made from wood (above) with a small hole at the side close to the bark of the tree.

All sorts of different nest sites may be used by wrens, such as a coconut with a hole in it (left) or a hanging flowerpot (above).

A more open nesting tray with a roof (above), may be used by American robins and phoebes if placed on the side of a house.

Birds need material to build and line their nests. A basket full of string, wool, hair, and feathers (above) will help them.

THE DIRECTORY
100 Song Birds

GROSBEAKS, FINCHES, BUNTINGS: *Fringillidae*

Small birds with short, conical bills. Most are arboreal, sparrows (also included in the group) are more terrestrial. Grosbeaks warble; finches tend to chirp; bunting songs are often high and lively; and sparrows have musical whistles.

BLACKBIRDS AND ORIOLES: *Icteridae*

Medium-sized birds with strong, pointed bills. Blackbirds have loud, coarse songs; orioles use piping whistles.

TANAGERS: *Thraupidae*

Birds of tropical origin; males are brilliantly colored and sing hoarse robin-like songs from tree-tops; also have dry, staccato calls.

HOW TO USE THE DIRECTORY

The great range of notes and rhythms on display in bird song can be confusing, but once mastered, the language adds a whole new dimension to bird study. This directory helps to do this, featuring the songs and calls of 100 songbirds, many of which can be attracted to your backyard or garden as breeding species. Winter visitors to the feeder, tempted by sensible natural food and cover, may stop by to feed or rest as well as those species on their spring and fall migrations.

Information on when and where all these birds sing is accompanied by interesting aspects of feeding and breeding behavior.

With the birds grouped in families, it is easy to make out the broad outline of any common song features for each group – for example the sweet, clear notes of the thrushes, the buzzy, wheezy notes of sparrows, and the thin high-pitched songs of many of the warblers.

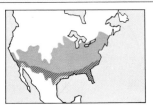

① Outlined maps of North America give detailed distribution information, including migratory patterns. The maps show summer distribution (in green), winter distribution (in diagonal hatching) and all year distribution (in green with diagonal hatching).

▢ Summer distribution

▨ Winter distribution

▨ All year distribution

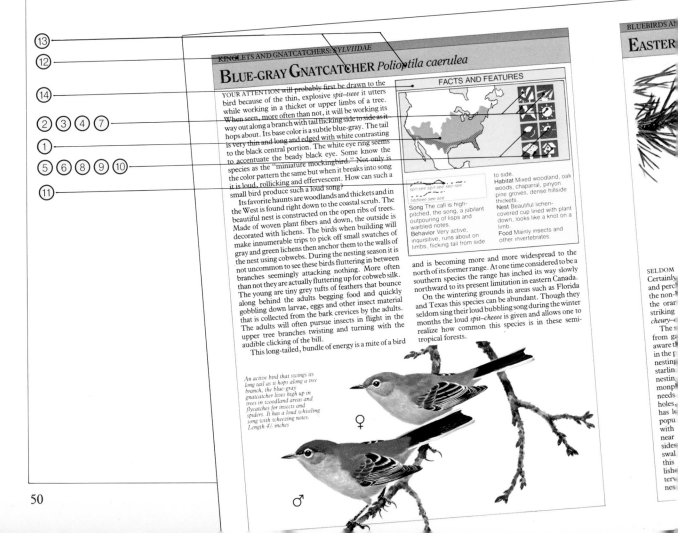

KINGLETS AND GNATCATCHERS: *SYLVIIDAE*

BLUE-GRAY GNATCATCHER *Polioptila caerulea*

YOUR ATTENTION will probably first be drawn to the bird because of the thin, explosive *spit–tseee* it utters while working in a thicket or upper limbs of a tree. When seen, more often than not, it will be working its way out along a branch with tail flicking side to side as it hops about. Its base color is a subtle blue-gray. The tail is very thin and long and edged with white contrasting to the black central portion. The white eye ring seems to accentuate the beady black eye. Some know the species as the "miniature mockingbird." Not only is the color pattern the same but when it breaks into song it is loud, rollicking and effervescent. How can such a small bird produce such a loud song?

Its favorite haunts are woodlands and thickets and in the West is found right down to the coastal scrub. The beautiful nest is constructed on the open ribs of trees. Made of woven plant fibers and down, the outside is decorated with lichens. The birds when building will make innumerable trips to pick off small swatches of gray and green lichens then anchor them to the walls of the nest using cobwebs. During the nesting season it is not uncommon to see these birds fluttering in between branches seemingly attacking nothing. More often than not they are actually fluttering up for cobweb silk. The young are tiny grey tufts of feathers that bounce along behind the adults begging food and quickly gobbling down larvae, eggs and other insect material that is collected from the bark crevices by the adults. The adults will often pursue insects in flight in the upper tree branches twisting and turning with the audible clicking of the bill.

This long-tailed, bundle of energy is a mite of a bird

An active bird that swings its long tail as it hops along a tree branch, the blue-gray gnatcatcher lives high up in trees in woodland areas and flycatches for insects and spiders. It has a loud whistling song with wheezing notes. Length 4½ inches

FACTS AND FEATURES

spit-see spit-see see-see

hddieee see see

Song The call is high-pitched, the song, a jubilant outpouring of lisps and warbled notes.
Behavior Very active, inquisitive, runs about on limbs, flicking tail from side to side.
Habitat Mixed woodland, oak woods, chaparral, pinyon pine groves, dense hillside thickets.
Nest Beautiful lichen-covered cup lined with plant down, looks like a knot on a limb.
Food Mainly insects and other invertebrates.

and is becoming more and more widespread to the north of its former range. At one time considered to be a southern species the range has inched its way slowly northward to its present limitation in eastern Canada.

On the wintering grounds in areas such as Florida and Texas this species can be abundant. Though they seldom sing their loud bubbling song during the winter months the loud *spit–cheeee* is given and allows one to realize how common this species is in these semi-tropical forests.

♀

♂

BLUEBIRDS AI

EASTER

SELDOM
Certainly
and perch
the non-
the orar
striking
cheury–
The s
from ga
aware t
in the p
nesting
starlin
nestin
monp
needs
holes,
has le
popu
with
near
sides
swal
this
lishe
ter
nes

② The forest and woodland symbol indicates that the bird is usually found in treed areas, including orchards and gardens.

 ③ The open country symbol includes grasslands, tundra, low scrub and bog.

 ④ The flight symbol indicates that the bird sings mainly in flight or has a typical flight song or call.

⑤ The nest box symbol indicates that the bird will use a nest box provided it is the right type and size.

 ⑥ The bird table symbol indicates that the bird can be attracted to a feeding area.

 ⑦ Sings all day.

 ⑧ Sings in the morning.

⑨ Sings in the afternoon or evening.

⑩ More than one "time of day" symbol may be ticked, for example when a bird may sing all day, but predominantly in the morning or evening.

⑪ Rhythm box; the rhythmic flow of a bird's song is given for each species using simple linear notation. The length of pause between notes depicts the rapidity of the song.
   The base components are as follows:

Rising pitch

Drop in pitch

Long note

Fast rising inflection and sudden drop

A rollercoasting effect

Very rapid

Long notes and long pauses

Short notes and long pauses

⑫ Family name, English and scientific.

⑬ Species name, English and scientific.

⑭ "Facts and features" box for easy reference, which contains a distribution map, song description and pattern, behavior, typical habitat, and nest and food information including types used to attract birds to the feeder.

SHES: TURDIDAE

UEBIRD *Sialia sialis*

♀

♂

A thrush with blue upperparts contrasting with rich rust below and a white underbelly, the bluebird is one of the best known songbirds in the US. It perches high up in trees and drops down to seize insects, then returning to its perch. It also eats fruits, berries and seeds. Length 7 inches

O ENDEARED itself to so many. one flying up from beside the road ncepost is a sight that excites even spectacular blue contrasting with ite of the underparts is a most n. The song is a short soft warble repeated.

luebirds is often the talk of the day o farmyard and most people are ot see as many bluebirds as they did things have affected the Bluebird's The introduction of the European is a main factor. Eviction from they man-made or natural, is com- ition, the species has very specific te, favorite sites being old trees with ireland. But a great deal of the East tureland and with it, the bluebird birds can however be encouraged set on posts fairly low to the ground edge but in a position that is open all itely such a site is also attractive to tree often usurp the nest box. To counter 'Bluebird Trails" have been estab- ge numbers of boxes are placed at in- habitats, affording a wide selection for herein lies the hope of the future for

this lovely bird, and indeed in many areas such as the Midwest and Southern Canada, the Bluebird is making a remarkable comeback. More "pieces of azure" to delight generations to come.

FACTS AND FEATURES

ta ta tee o ta ta toe lee
Song A mellow series of notes usually sung at low level, sounds like a gutteral warbling.
Behavior Flutters about in open areas when feeding, often drops to ground to feed; has a very buoyant

flight.
Habitat Open woodland edges, farmland, orchards gardens.
Nest A cup of twigs placed in a natural cavity, abandoned nest hole or nest box.
Food Mainly insects with some berries, and seeds.

83

EASTERN KINGBIRD *Tyrannus tyrannus*

FLYCATCHERS IN GENERAL pose a problem in identification for the beginning birder. Therefore, it is welcome to find one that is easy to identify by sight, sound and action. It seems that everything about this bird is unique enough to make it stand out. Although the color pattern is gray above with a much darker head and white underparts, the white band on the end of the tail is found in no other North American flycatcher.

Its favorite perch is atop a tree in an orchard, garden, open field edge or along a waterway. Any open area may attract this species. From its perch it sallies forth with stiffened wingbeats and as it makes this quivering flight it calls *zeek–zeek–zeek* and follows with *kip–kip–kip–dzypper–dzypper*. These are display flights which contrast with the more directed flight of a bird darting off a perch to capture a flying insect. When completing the display flight or when incensed by the presence of a predator in the area the crown feathers are raised and it is usually then – and only then – that the fiery rust-red crown feathers can be seen. It is this crown that gives the group its name of "kingbirds."

The nest is a bulky structure of sticks placed in the crotch of a larger tree usually well off the ground. In defence of this site the Kingbird shows no fear. It dive-bombs ground predators from the air, often touching the backs of cats, foxes and the like. In the air it will defend itself against any trespasser, including crows and hawks which are harried with swooping maneuvers aimed at their backs. Even a passing eagle will be targeted by a bird bent on defending its area.

One of its favorite food items are bees and if an apiary lies within one's territory it will spend endless hours inflicting heavy damage on colonies much to the chagrin of the beekeeper. But overall, the benefits of having this species far outweigh its few bad habits.

FACTS AND FEATURES

kazeeh kazeeh-kip-kip

dzypper dzypper

Song A loud series of twitters and harsh notes.
Behavior Flies out from tree tops on quivering wings; usually solitary; very defensive of nesting territory.

Habitat Open areas such as field edges, forest clearing, farmlands, orchards, gardens; often near water.
Nest Large loose cup of grasses, weeds and other plant material lined with plant down.
Food Winged insects especially bees, occasionally berries.

The eastern kingbird is most easily identified by its black tail, white underparts, and narrow white wing bars. A small orange patch on the crown is partly concealed and difficult to see in the field. Length 8 inches

EASTERN WOOD PEWEE *Contopus virens*

WALKING THROUGH THE DRY UPLAND woods of early summer the long drawn-out *peeeee–weee* is a familiar sound. The vernacular and common names of many of the flycatchers are based on the song or the habitat in which they are found. Taking time to track the singer down will lead to a small, drab brown bird sitting in a vertical position, often on the dead stub of a branch fairly high off the ground. Two wing bars can be clearly seen and the orange yellow of the lower mandible clinches the identification. The bird uses the perch as a command post for spotting insects and quickly darts out to grab them before returning to its favored spot.

When not in song the bird may be difficult to see due to its sedentary ways. The nest is even more difficult to locate and consists of a small cup of plant fibers covered with lichens, fibers held in place by cobwebs. It is placed on the upper surface of the limb and usually at a bend, therefore assuming the features of a small knot on the limb.

The species is interesting in that it varies its song depending on the time of day. Most of the day it is a repetitious *pee–a–wee* which at times is followed by a slurred *pee–oooo*. However, the early morning and low light levels of late afternoon are marked by an explosive part to the song, with a sharp additional A sharp, rising *a–deedit*.

The range of the Eastern Pewee abuts that of the western wood pewee on the western side of the Great Plains. Although their ranges do overlap slightly in some areas, interbreeding has not been reported. In the field the two species are virtually impossible to distinguish, the only separating factor being the harsh slurred *feeear* call of the western wood peewee, mainly uttered during the early morning or late afternoon.

Unlike its near lookalike, the eastern phoebe, the eastern wood pewee sits motionless and does not pump its tail; it also has longer wings and a pale lower mandible. Length 6¼ inches

FACTS AND FEATURES

peee-a-weeeee pee-a-weeeee

Song A loud, long drawn out and often mournful sound with a rising inflection at the end.
Behavior Sedentary, calls from broken branch stub; frequents the area just below the tree canopy.

Habitat Woodlands, orchards.
Nest Shallow well disguised cup of mosses and lichens, looks like a knot of a limb.
Food Insects which are snapped up as it sallies forth from a dead limb perch.

EASTERN PHOEBE *Sayornis phoebe*

WHEN THE NORTHEASTERN woodlands are still dun gray but hints of buds tint the branches reddish and warm sunlit pockets host the first dancing masses of soldierflies, the emphatic call of *fee-beep – fee-beep* marks the arrival of the first flycatcher of the spring, the Eastern Phoebe. Beginning birders very often confuse the *fee–bee* call of the black-capped chickadee with this species. However, whereas the chickadee phrase is drawn out, mournful and drops in pitch, the Phoebe's is explosive and rises sharply. When found the songster is usually in a bolt upright position, tail bobbing up and down and rapidly looking about for insects. Gray above and pale below, the head shows very dark in contrast to the back. Lack of eye ring and wingbars also helps separate it from other lookalikes.

This is one species that has adapted well to the structures of man. Although they can still be seen nesting within the mixed upland woods on cliff over-hangs and rocky outcrops they do seem to fit right into the suburban situation. Understreet culverts are favorite sites, as is any bridge near suitable woodland habitat. Buildings are used and overhangs of barns and

FACTS AND FEATURES

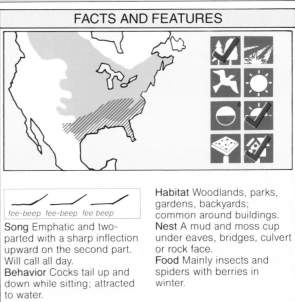

Song Emphatic and two-parted with a sharp inflection upward on the second part. Will call all day.
Behavior Cocks tail up and down while sitting; attracted to water.

Habitat Woodlands, parks, gardens, backyards; common around buildings.
Nest A mud and moss cup under eaves, bridges, culvert or rock face.
Food Mainly insects and spiders with berries in winter.

garages are also favored. The nest is a well made cup of mud, rootlets and fibers and usually is covered with mosses. If it is in a well-protected site it will be upgraded and used for many years in succession.

In the fall young birds will show a marked lemon tint to the underparts, and buff edged wingbars that are indistinct. No other flycatcher at this time shows these features. Hardy, they linger well into the fall and some even attempt overwintering, shifting to a berry diet.

A summer visitor to the Northeast and a winter resident of the Southeast, the eastern phoebe can be found in a wide variety of habitats. It is almost exclusively an insect eater but in the fall or under stress it will eat berries. Length 7 inches

SAY'S PHOEBE *Sayornis saya*

FACTS AND FEATURES

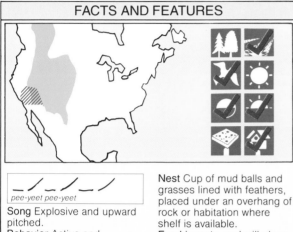

This bird is common in plains and in canyons where it perches on fences, bushes and boulders. It can be identified by its black tail and rust-colored belly and undertail feathers. Length 7-8 inches

pee-yeet pee-yeet

Song Explosive and upward pitched.
Behavior Active and restless; flutters to ground to feed; bobs tail as it sits; will sing in flight.
Habitat Open and rocky country.

Nest Cup of mud balls and grasses lined with feathers, placed under an overhang of rock or habitation where shelf is available.
Food Insects, and will glean spiders from rock surfaces, berries taken in winter.

THE ALASKAN TUNDRA is marked by wide rocky stream beds and sharp canyons, cut away over millions of years. In such a setting the Say's Phoebe reaches the northern limit of its range, a range that extends from the edge of the Arctic Circle south to the Mexican border in Arizona and then down well into Mexico. Throughout, the bird prefers the dry, open areas, canyons and cliffs that form an interlacing network over this vast range.

Within these canyons the explosive *pee–yeet* call is magnified and echoed, making the exact location of the singing bird difficult to spot. When sighted, the bird is found perched atop a boulder or scrub-bush pumping its tail up and down and often fanning it open with rapid flicks.

Gray in over-all appearance, the top of the head is capped with a darker gray, the tail is black, and the underbelly from the breast line to undertail coverts a soft orange color. The song is often delivered *pit – pit pit – pit seeer* after the explosive call notes. Near the nest site, the song is very often delivered as the bird hovers in the air, wings aflutter, before returning to its roost spot. In underdeveloped areas, cliff faces and rocky outcrops are the selected sites to place the nest. In developed areas they, like the other phoebes, often select a flat site under the overhang of a roof, under a bridge or, in the Southwest, even in old mine shafts. The nest is typically phoebe, made of mud pellets, grass and plant fibers, and very often lined with feathers. A highly migratory species, it overwinters in Mexico and further south, although stray birds, mainly immatures, do from time to time show up on the Eastern seaboard.

GREAT CRESTED FLYCATCHER *Myiarchus crinitus*

THIS SPECIES IS A COMMON RESIDENT of open wood-lands in the eastern half of the United States. However, because it prefers the upper areas of oaks, hickories, and maples it is not always that easy to see. Indeed, the distinctive *weeerrrup* call is often the only give-away of this bird's presence. An active flycatcher, it can be tracked down with perseverance and spotted through gaps in the forest canopy. More often than not it is found sitting on a dead stub, within the canopy, in an upright position and constantly moving its head around in search of insect prey. Should any other birds be in the vicinity it will often erect its crest and stretch its neck, bobbing it up and down in a defensive posture.

It is a large flycatcher and distinctively marked. It has brown upper parts with a crest that can be erect or suppressed. The throat down the mid-chest is dark gray and this contrasts to lemon-yellow underparts. The tail and wing are marked with cinnamon, best seen when spread.

This is one of the few flycatchers in our area that uses a natural cavity for nesting. Old woodpecker holes are also used and the birds will also take readily to nesting boxes placed in their territory. The nest is of sticks, grasses, leaves and other plant material. One unique feature of the nest is the inclusion of snakeskins within the lining. In situations where they nest

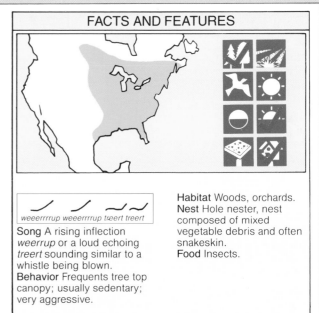

FACTS AND FEATURES

weeerrrrup weeerrrrup træert treert

Song A rising inflection *weerrup* or a loud echoing *treert* sounding similar to a whistle being blown.
Behavior Frequents tree top canopy; usually sedentary; very aggressive.

Habitat Woods, orchards.
Nest Hole nester, nest composed of mixed vegetable debris and often snakeskin.
Food Insects.

near habitation paper may be used as a replacement.

With a lack of winter food supply in the North, the population migrates south to winter in southern Florida (where there is a significant population), Mexico and on through Central and South America.

Often seen in the higher branches of trees in deciduous woodlands and orchards, this large bird has a bushy crest and a large broad bill. It has a rust-red tail, especially visible from below, gray throat, and a yellow belly and undertail. Length 8½ inches.

OLIVE-SIDED FLYCATCHER *Nuttallornis borealis*

THE FLYCATCHERS IN GENERAL are a rather difficult group to separate in the field – so many birds are so similar that relying on call is the normal way to clinch an identification. However, the Olive-sided Flycatcher makes it easy on both accounts – sight and sound.

The song once heard is not forgotten, a very clear and distinctive *quick–three–beers* often followed by a series of *pit–pit–pit* call notes. The bird's favored breeding haunts are the cool boglands and evergreen forests of the north. More often than not the song alerts the birder. The best way to locate the songster is to scan all the tall dead spires of spruce. There, perched on the very top in upright posture will be seen this large flycatcher. For its size it has a fairly short tail and large head; to the sides of the rump area can usually be seen two white feather tufts; the center of the breast is a dull white that runs up into a white throat area; and the sides of the breast present a distinct field mark. Smudgy gray, they wrap in toward the central breast giving the bird the appearance of wearing a "vest." It may dart out into the air to grab insects but will quickly return to the spire to call and sing. Flicking its wings and twisting atop the spire's peak, its voice repeats over and over *quick–three–beers – pitpit – quick–three–beers*.

The nest, a cup-like structure placed in an evergreen, is covered with mosses or lichens. In areas where the green draping mats of *Usnea* lichen is found this is normally used to cover the outside of the nest, making its detection almost impossible.

With the onset of fall the birds head south on a rather long journey. During this time they appear in a variety of habitats and usually are silent. However, they remain drawn to the tops of dead snags in open areas. Their journey takes them many hundreds of miles away to their wintering grounds, the volcanic hillsides and cool ravines of Columbia and Peru. Here, they again sit high above the forest uttering their low *pit–pit–pit* call notes. Rarely is the distinctive call given, but when heard, the birder's mind quickly shifts to the evergreen spires of the northern breeding grounds, so many miles away.

A large, stocky flycatcher with a short tail, this bird has an olive-green back, white underparts and dark green, streaked flanks. White tufts on either side of its rump show well in flight. It prefers tall coniferous forests or in clusters of trees in bogs. Length 7½ inches.

FACTS AND FEATURES

quick-three-beers

Song A very distinct and clear three parted series, the phrase is drawn out. Song delivered from the top of a tree.
Behavior Sings from an exposed perch; strongly defends nest site.

Habitat Dead trees in northern coniferous forest, especially spruce in north of range and pitch pine in the south.
Nest Shallow cup of twigs placed well out on slender limb of conifer.
Food Insects.

VERMILLION FLYCATCHER *Pyrocephalus rubinus*

IT HAS BEEN LIKENED TO A "glowing ember," a "living jewel" and numerous other embodiments of beauty. For years I have led trips to the Southwest and invariably, the Vermillion Flycatcher is in the "top 10 most wanted birds." The male is the showpiece, glowing vermillion with black back, wings and tail and a jet black mask. But even the female with her mouse-brown back, striped underparts and blush rouge sides and underbelly is attractive. During the breeding season the male will often do a flutter flight when the female is near and then the soft, musical song of *hit–a–see hit–a–see* can be heard.

When found they are usually fairly approachable. Sitting atop a dead snag they have a habit of constantly pumping and fanning their tail, their head jerking about as they scan for insects. When spotted they flutter off into the air or drop to the ground, each time increasing the amount of vermillion to be seen.

Though found in a variety of habitats they prefer areas in the generally arid Southwest where there is constant water. Stream beds, river edges, water-towers, cow drinking troughs – all are attractive.

Made of plant fibers and covered with lichens, the nest is tucked so tightly into the fork of a tree crotch that only the upper edge can usually be seen. If it weren't for

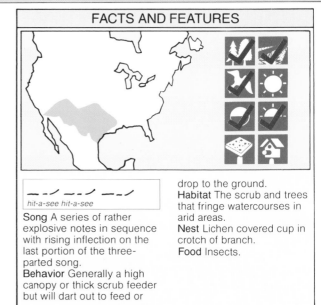

FACTS AND FEATURES

hit-a-see hit-a-see

Song A series of rather explosive notes in sequence with rising inflection on the last portion of the three-parted song.
Behavior Generally a high canopy or thick scrub feeder but will dart out to feed or drop to the ground.
Habitat The scrub and trees that fringe watercourses in arid areas.
Nest Lichen covered cup in crotch of branch.
Food Insects.

the comings and goings of the male in attending the young, finding the nest would be nearly impossible!

The male vermillion flycatcher is unmistakable with its bright red crown and underparts. The adult female has gray-brown plumage above, a finely streaked white throat and breast and a pink belly and undertail. It lives in thickets near water in the Southwest. Length 6 inches

WILLOW FLYCATCHER *Empidonax traillii*

One of several similar Empidonax species, the willow flycatcher has a pale eye ring and a dark olive-brown head. As its name suggests, it prefers willow as well as alder thickets. Length 5½ inches

THE FLYCATCHER GROUP to which this species belongs is one that challenges even the more advanced birders and can leave the beginning birder completely frustrated. All seem to be olive and gray with eye rings and wingbars. Prolonged study, however, can lead to at least some success in identification. If the bird in question calls, then the identification can usually be made without hesitation. The Willow Flycatcher is no exception to the rule. Its song is most diagnostic: a wheezy *fitz–bew* with the emphasis on the first part. Note, however, that it lacks the well defined eye-ring of its look-alike relatives, has a white throat that contrasts to the olive tinted breast and the underbelly shows a yellowish cast.

The species frequents a wide variety of habitat over its extensive range. Pastureland, brushy clearings, stream edges, orchards and on up to rolling mountain meadows. In general it is to be found in a dryer situation than its closest look-alike, the alder flycatcher. In fact, for many years the two species were considered to be one. As the name implies it feeds on flying insects and can usually be found sitting in a prominent perch on its territory from which it darts out to snap up an insect.

The nest is a well-woven structure of plant fibers and covered with silken materials affixed to the nest by spiderwebbing. It is placed in the crotch of a limb in a small tree or shrub.

In migration these birds are likely to appear in almost any habitat. They sit without moving for long periods and are often overlooked. During this time listen for a liquid *whit–whit* call and you could be well rewarded.

FACTS AND FEATURES

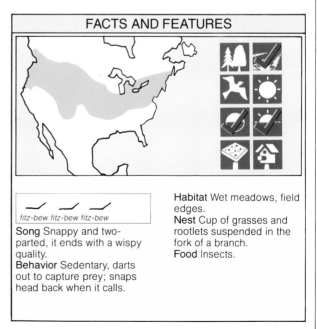

fitz-bew fitz-bew fitz-bew

Song Snappy and two-parted, it ends with a wispy quality.
Behavior Sedentary, darts out to capture prey; snaps head back when it calls.

Habitat Wet meadows, field edges.
Nest Cup of grasses and rootlets suspended in the fork of a branch.
Food Insects.

HORNED LARK *Eremophila alpestris*

SHELLEY WROTE HIS ODE but no one has done the same for the Horned Lark, yet the sweet twittering song drifting down from a clear blue sky in an open field or along a beach certainly is moving enough to elicit the poetic feeling in almost anyone. The Horned Lark is a common bird throughout North America except in the very limits of the Southeast. It nests from far above the Arctic Circle on down through Central America.

With such a vast range (it can also be found throughout most of Europe south to North Africa) it shows a wide range of color variability. However, the base pattern is always present – tawny brown with distinct mask through the eyes, a black bib and two horn-like feather groups in breeding plumage. They scuttle about very low to the ground in search of seeds, grass and sedge seeds in particular, and are as at home on a wind-blown rocky ridge of the Alaskan Range to a freshly turned over farm field in Texas. In all these areas the nest is the same: a small scrape lined with grasses and usually placed at the base of a grass or sedge clump. The young birds are wonderful little balls of feathers that are black and white in color often giving a zebra pattern in appearance.

Overwintering flocks moving south to the US from their tundra breeding grounds usually head for wind-swept beaches or farm fields. In such places as south-

FACTS AND FEATURES

peet tweedle ee dee deet/
peet tweedle ee dee deet

Song A soft tinkling series of notes usually delivered from high overhead.
Behavior Sings in the air and on the ground; shuffles about when feeding; gregarious.

Habitat Tundra, alpine areas, shorelines, agricultural land.
Nest Cup of grasses on the ground, at the base of a rock or clump of grass.
Food Seeds, insects and other small invertebrates.

ern California it is not uncommon to see fields with thousands of these birds. These disperse by late winter and in early spring the tinkling song is once again heard over a significant portion of the northern hemisphere.

Horned larks vary in color from a pale gray to a reddish brown, but they all have the same distinctive black breast mark and facial pattern and many have a yellow face. Length 7¼ inches

PURPLE MARTIN *Progne subis*

FACTS AND FEATURES

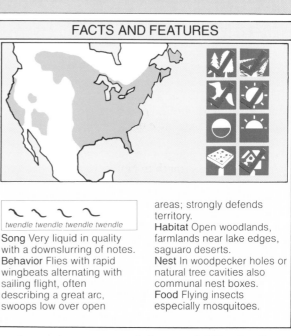

twendle twendle twendle twendle

Song Very liquid in quality with a downslurring of notes.
Behavior Flies with rapid wingbeats alternating with sailing flight, often describing a great arc, swoops low over open areas; strongly defends territory.
Habitat Open woodlands, farmlands near lake edges, saguaro deserts.
Nest In woodpecker holes or natural tree cavities also communal nest boxes.
Food Flying insects especially mosquitoes.

The largest of the swallows in North America, the male of the species is an iridescent blue-purple. The purple martin eats insects, especially mosquitoes, which it catches on the wing and lives where there is a large "swoop area" as well as water and housing. It can be attracted to specially built communal nesting sites. Length 5 inches

NO NORTH AMERICAN SPECIES relies so much on man for housing as does the Purple Martin. Prior to the development of our continent, literally from coast to coast, there were natural tree cavities and rock crevices in which the Purple Martin could nest. Rock crevices remain a last resort in some areas and colonies do inhabit the giant trees of western forests that have spacious fissures in them. But in most regions man-made structures are the only sites occupied – some are truly massive, accommodating over 1,000 pairs. Some cities have adopted them and hold festivals in their honor and large bird gourd complexes throughout towns welcome the birds' return each spring. Even in such organized situations they are pressured by starlings, however, and the western populations in particular are being evicted from old woodpecker nesting holes and the like.

Perhaps the Purple Martin's most desirable quality lies in its reputation as a mosquito eater; people will go to great lengths to encourage anything that can reduce the impact of these annoying insects. In addition the birds are beautiful; the males sport an all purple iridescent plumage and they have a rich loud, liquid song. In flight they are graceful and fun to watch as they execute spectacular aerial maneuvers.

As an exclusive insect eater it moves south for the winter, not just a short way but on into South America where its complete winter area has as yet to be fully described. They return north early, a few birds trickling in to signal the arrival of the main influx within a couple of weeks. The houses are checked and first investigations made. Often if left up and not cleaned out house sparrows or starlings will already be in occupancy and thwart the martins' investigations. So proper maintenance is a must. By early April the skies are again alive with birds as they swoop low over the fields and water.

TREE SWALLOW *Iridoprocne bicolor*

SWIRLING MASSES OF THOUSANDS of these birds are not an uncommon sight in the fall as they head south on migration bound for the extreme southern portions of the United States, Mexico and Central America. At times power lines and buildings are totally covered by their masses. En route fruiting bushes, such as bayberry, bend to the ground under the weight, as every berry is picked clean. In the Everglades flocks estimated in the millions can darken the sky as they move from one site to another.

It is obvious that this bird is a very successful nester. Natural cavities and birdhouses are taken readily. The birds favor open fields, meadows, farmyards and coastal marshlands. Flooded swamplands with dead trees riddled with old woodpecker holes are another favored nesting site. The loud repeated twitterings at these sites is an early spring ritual.

The birds show iridescent green backs with the green turning into black which passes under the eye and onto the cheek. This allows rapid separation from the look-alike violet-green swallow. The underparts are a pure white. Females have drabber backs and the young birds are brown-backed. Swirls of these birds at times seem to appear from nowhere as they drop from the sky to skim the water to drink or swoop up insects. This type of surprise arrival and splashing in the water led early observers to feel that the swallows may have overwintered in the mud

FACTS AND FEATURES

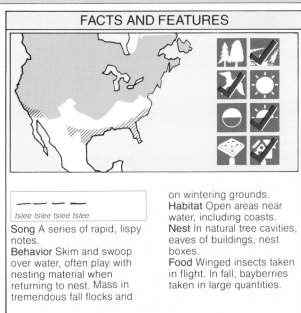

-- -- -- --
tslee tslee tslee tslee

Song A series of rapid, lispy notes.
Behavior Skim and swoop over water, often play with nesting material when returning to nest. Mass in tremendous fall flocks and on wintering grounds.
Habitat Open areas near water, including coasts.
Nest In natural tree cavities, eaves of buildings, nest boxes.
Food Winged insects taken in flight. In fall, bayberries taken in large quantities.

on the lake's bottom! When gathering material for the nest cavity it is not uncommon to see birds playing with feathers that will be used to line the nest. It is at this time the swallows' true mastery of the air can be appreciated as they drop and swoop flicking the feather about and keeping it aloft in "play."

This glossy blue-green swallow prefers to live in open areas near water. It feeds by seizing winged insects in flight. In fall, it migrates in large groups to Florida. On the way the swallows swirl in flocks over fields and swoop en masse to feed on bayberries. Length 5½ inches

GRAY JAY *Perisoreus canadensis*

HIKING IN NORTHERN CONIFEROUS FORESTS among evergreens capped with puffs of snow that sag the branches in long sweeping skirts, one often hears a clear hollow whistling sound – *teelawoo wheeoooo chuck chuck*. One only need to pause and wait and soon you will be investigated by the most inquisitive of the northwoods' birds, the Gray Jay. It looks like an overgrown chickadee with muted grays and whites and seems more fluff than substance. With wide wings quickly flicking in and out, they glide roller-coaster fashion from tree to tree as they approach. At nearly 1ft long, they are impressive birds and will work in very close to inspect any intruder into their world and, more importantly, to check if there is any food available. They show no shyness. I have had birds hop onto my shoulder and literally pluck pieces of bread from between my hand and mouth. This tameness is not shown by any other North American bird, not even the friendly chickadee group.

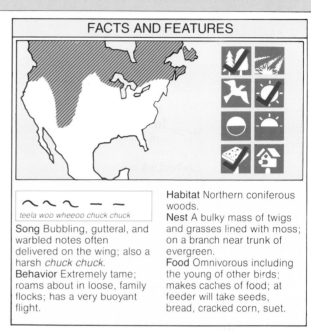

FACTS AND FEATURES

teela woo wheeoo chuck chuck

Song Bubbling, gutteral, and warbled notes often delivered on the wing; also a harsh *chuck chuck*.
Behavior Extremely tame; roams about in loose, family flocks; has a very buoyant flight.

Habitat Northern coniferous woods.
Nest A bulky mass of twigs and grasses lined with moss; on a branch near trunk of evergreen.
Food Omnivorous including the young of other birds; makes caches of food; at feeder will take seeds, bread, cracked corn, suet.

If juveniles are present, note how deep sooty-colored they are and the bright yellow of the mouth gape. Always begging for food they follow the foraging flock about with hope of effortlessly obtaining a meal. Their long interaction with hikers, campers and trappers of the North is typified by their many common names: camp robber, whiskey jack and camp follower are but a few. During severe winters they do move south slightly, which allows more people the opportunity to get to know one of the boldest and friendliest birds of the northern forest.

A bold, inquisitive bird that lives in woods and often visits campsites for food scraps, the gray jay has fluffy gray and white plumage, a short bill and a fairly long tail. Its color and lack of a crest help distinguish it from the Clark's nutcracker. Young birds have sooty gray plumage and a pale bill. Length 11½ inches

BLUE JAY *Cyanocitta cristata*

The blue jay is a bold, aggressive bird that will plunder other birds' nests, pester hawks and owls and even chase a cat. It needs no attracting to the birdfeeder as it will eat anything it finds there and will always find a way to get at the food. It prefers oak and pine forests where it finds acorns, nuts, insects and small animals to feed on. Length 11 inches

LOUD, BOLD, BRASH, COLORFUL. A myriad of adjectives can be used to describe this well-known bird of eastern North America. Its cohabitation with man and antics at the bird-feeding station makes it a familiar species of parks, backyards, even in the trees that line the streets of the largest cities. Blue Jays always seem to be there in all types of weather. To the birder from Europe it is a species on their "must see" list. This is accomplished very quickly upon their arrival at the airport. To the native birder or backyard feeding station operator, the jays' antics are often a source of dismay. At the feeder they bully and fill their mouths to overflowing. They take this hoarded loot off to an old bird's nest or some other site and hide it for future ingestion. They can quickly clean a feeding tray before the more "desirable" birds get a chance to visit. Afield, they are notorious nest robbers, often cleaning out the young of all the birds nesting in their vicinity. In addition they are the alert system for the woodlands. All one need do is enter an area with jays, and the alert is given for all other birds to hear no matter how secretive you are.

Their vocal repertoire is amazing. From low guttural notes that one can hear but a few feet away (called a whisper song), to the loud screams of *jay–jay–jay* that give them their name. They call like red-shouldered hawks, flickers, goshawks and other birds of their area. Thrown in are sounds from a frog croaking to the familiar clothesline being reeled in. Never a dull

moment with this species. And they are beautiful – the brilliance of blue offset by white spotting and a lovely necklace of black running to the edge of the erect crest. The female is marked identically except for white wing markings. Too often a bird such as the jay is so common that we consider it a pest species and fail to take time to admire its beauty.

FACTS AND FEATURES

jay-jay-jay tweelee tweelee tweelee

Song Besides the loud, harsh *jay-jay* it has a wide range of notes, soft whisper songs of low whistles, loud mimicry calls of hawks and two parted explosive note sequences.
Behavior Loud, bold; moves about in groups.
Habitat Forest, woodland (especialy with oaks), orchards, parks, gardens.
Nest A bulky cup of sticks, grapevine, in limb crotch of oak, maple or large shrub.
Food Omnivorous especially acorns and beechnuts; readily comes to feeder.

AMERICAN CROW *Corvus brachyrhynchos*

Well-known for its large size, black color and caw-caw-caw *call, the crow lives in a wide variety of habitats throughout the country. It likes to eat corn but has a varied diet including both animal and vegetable matter. Length 18 inches*

IN THE MIDST of winter's grip when snow crunches underfoot with cold extremes and words condense into ice fog to freeze on one's cap, the crisp clear calls of the crow seem as much a part of a northern walk as rolling fields and dairy barns.

The crow's ability to learn is legendary and studies have shown that they are among the most intelligent of all bird species. Besides its reputation as a "villain" it is also known for its intricate behavioral patterns. It is one species that almost seems to be able to think through a situation and weigh the outcome. It is a very social species and roosts of thousands are not uncommon. When foraging for food working parties scour the area while one bird is always on lookout for danger. Every aspect of wariness and cunning is used in obtaining food, and being an omnivore anything is taken. Be it stealing from a smaller bird, getting food from a dumpsite, grabbing unattended food or actually working to find it, it is certain that most of the time the crow will meet with success.

Though intelligent there is no truth that splitting a crow's tongue will allow it to talk. They can mimic sounds and words and have a wide repertoire of gurgles, harsh yells, and bubbling sounds in addition to the familiar *caw caw caw*. The nest is constructed very early in the year before any leafing (in the Northeast) and the young are often comical, leaving the nest in pursuit of parents and begging for food.

FACTS AND FEATURES

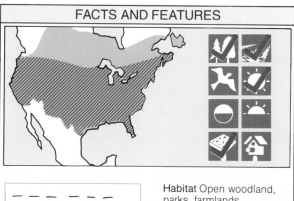

caw-caw-caw caw-caw-caw

Song Loud and distinctive.
Behavior Moves in organized groups; often roosts in tremendous numbers. Very adaptive.

Habitat Open woodland, parks, farmlands, rangelands.
Nest A bulky mass of sticks in crotch of tree.
Food Omnivorous.

BLACK-CAPPED CHICKADEE *Parus atricapillus*

A familiar visitor to the birdfeeder, the chickadee will also eat berries and insects garnered from the branches and trunks of trees and from the underside of leaves. It has a black cap and bib, a drawn out mating call similar to a phoebe's and a full measure of curiosity which causes it to move about and investigate. Length 5 inches

TO THE BACKYARD BIRDWATCHER the Black-capped Chickadee is the life of the feeding station or tray. Their happy call of *chick–a–dee–dee* signifies their presence often before they are seen. With consistency of placing out food they quickly learn the routine and arrive at the same time each day to "walk to the feeder with you." Their inquisitiveness and trust make them a species that is easy to attract to the outstretched hand with food, and so confiding have some become that they land on the head and shoulders of the person with food.

Even in the forest situation they often come in close to inspect the woodland intruder. If one makes low squeaking notes with pursed lips or by kissing the back of the hand the birds will come remarkably close to investigate what they feel is another species scolding a predator. They work about you peering down with jet black beady eyes and the black of the cap raised, giving it a jaunty forward pitch and the black bib pulsating in and out as they call. Once no predator is found they quickly go back to foraging up trunks, under bark flaps, along limbs or even hovering under leaves with rapid wingbeats. They often forage with close "relatives" such as tufted titmouse or white-breasted nuthatch making up a very effective hunting party. In the fall they will associate with the moving groups of migrant warblers and thereby alert the birder to the presence of birds that might otherwise be overlooked.

In the spring their true song is heard – a drawn out *feee–beeee*. For the uninitiated it sounds like it should be a phoebe, but it is the chickadee on its territory or looking for a mate. The nest is a natural cavity, a bird box, or if the tree is soft enough a cavity excavated by the birds themselves. The nest may produce six young that actively forage with the adults within a few weeks of hatching.

Though large populations move down from the coldest parts of the North for the winter, a good number of the birds remain resident in their areas throughout the year. Indeed, it is the only species recorded on every Maine Christmas count throughout the years it has been run.

FACTS AND FEATURES

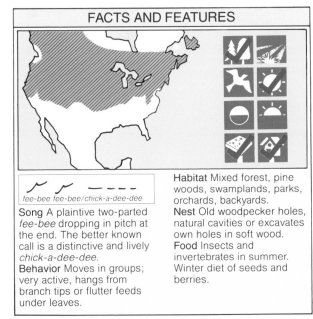

fee-bee fee-bee/chick-a-dee-dee

Song A plaintive two-parted *fee-bee* dropping in pitch at the end. The better known call is a distinctive and lively *chick-a-dee-dee*.
Behavior Moves in groups; very active, hangs from branch tips or flutter feeds under leaves.

Habitat Mixed forest, pine woods, swamplands, parks, orchards, backyards.
Nest Old woodpecker holes, natural cavities or excavates own holes in soft wood.
Food Insects and invertebrates in summer. Winter diet of seeds and berries.

BOREAL CHICKADEE *Parus hudsonicus*

CANADA AND ALASKA with their extensive boreal forests play host to this species year-round. In the lower 48 states, outside of northern New England and the Cascades of the Northwest, it remains a visitor from time to time on a most unpredictable timetable. In some years irruptions carry scattered birds or small groups far south of their normal extension.

In appearance it is similar to the well known black-capped chickadee except that the top of the head is brown and the sides a frosted tawny color. The call is a distinct *seek–a–day–day* with a strong accent on the ending syllables. As with all members of the chickadee complex they love to wander about in loose flocks investigating every nook and cranny of the trees' bark and foliage.

Because of its desire to stay within the evergreens it is rarely encountered in a garden situation unless it lies within the boreal area. Under these circumstances they will come to a feeder for peanut hearts, peanut butter and sunflower seeds. In the lower 48 states it will often put in an appearance at a feeder and stay for the winter's duration, being a single bird well out of territory and whose only contact is the black-capped chickadees coming in to feed. With the onset of spring, they will join the movement of chickadee flocks northward and return to their evergreen world. All birds of the family Paridae are hole nesters and this species is no exception. A delightful sight in the boreal forest is to see a flock of little brown balls of fluff following their parents about, trying to be the first recipient for a food morsel.

FACTS AND FEATURES

seek-a-day-day/

see-you

Song Call is most familiar, repetitious with accented rise at the end; song is a repeated warble.
Behavior Roams in small flocks; hangs from limb tips.

Habitat Northern coniferous forest.
Nest Natural cavities, old woodpecker holes, excavates own hole in soft wood.
Food Insects, their eggs and larvae and spiders.

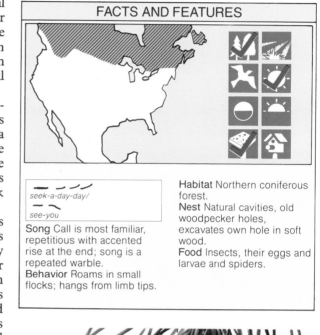

Its brown cap, brown back, white cheeks and brown flanks distinguish the boreal chickadee from all other chickadees. It also has a distinctive slow seek-a-day-day *call. It lives in coniferous and mixed woodlands and may forage elsewhere during hard winters. Length 5½ inches*

TUFTED TITMOUSE *Parus bicolor*

A gray bird with a head crest, dark button eyes and orange-tinted sides, the tufted titmouse is a near relative of the chickadee. Like the chickadee, it is inquisitive, relatively tame and a frequent visitor to the birdfeeder. The bulk of its diet, however, is insect matter. Length 6 inches

A CALL LIKE A PERSON whistling for their dog *wheeee-o-weet*, or a loud *peter-peter-peter* in rapid succession indicates the presence of this bird. It is one of those species that one invariably hears before seeing it. When located it is rarely alone but in the company of other titmice or their close relatives, the black-capped chickadees and white-breasted nuthatch. The party moves rapidly through the trees covering every nook and cranny in search of food.

Upland woods, evergreen forests, lowland swamps, backyards and formal gardens, all are the haunts of this gray little juggernaut. When finally seen the beady little black eye stands out below the distinct crest. Basically all gray above and white below, the flanks show a rusty coloration. In Texas the form called the black-crested titmouse occurs with a white forehead and a coal-black crest.

It nests in natural tree cavities, old woodpecker holes and in holes excavated in the soft wood of a dead tree. It will also take readily to nesting boxes placed at the wood edge or within the wooded part of a large garden. A permanent resident throughout their range they have slowly expanded northward over the last 30 years. One factor adding to their expansion has undoubtedly been feeding stations. In the winter, populations take up residence near feeders and will be daily visitors, with key periods of dependence occurring during storms that are several days in duration.

FACTS AND FEATURES

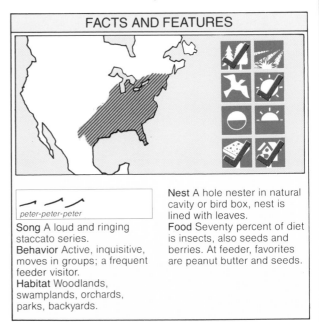

peter-peter-peter

Song A loud and ringing staccato series.
Behavior Active, inquisitive, moves in groups; a frequent feeder visitor.
Habitat Woodlands, swamplands, orchards, parks, backyards.

Nest A hole nester in natural cavity or bird box, nest is lined with leaves.
Food Seventy percent of diet is insects, also seeds and berries. At feeder, favorites are peanut butter and seeds.

PLAIN TITMOUSE *Parus inornatus*

IN THE OAK WOODLANDS OF coastal California a distinctive *tick–see–day–day* call often leads the East Coast birder in pursuit of what they believe will be a chickadee. In its place will be found a plain, drab brownish titmouse! As the name implies this species is totally without distinguishing features other than the distinct titmouse crest. Resident and fairly common within these oak woodlands they seem to prefer to work in batches, at the bases of trees or very often hopping about on the ground itself. In the spring, as the brown hillsides of California come into bloom and begin greening, the loud *weety weety weety* song can be heard echoing through the woods. Another race of this species lives on the other side of the Sierra Nevada, an inhabitant of juniper and pinyon pine forests. The call of this race is the same, but the color instead of being a drab brown is a lighter mousey gray.

As with the rest of the family this titmouse is very active and moves about in small bands with other related species. They take great joy in the discovery of a predator, such as a western screech owl or pygmy owl and will scold and flit about it for some time. These discoveries are often made as they are taking food to hide in some tree crevice or cavity. Peering in with the jet-bead eye they see the features of a

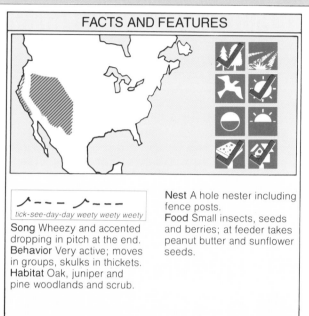

FACTS AND FEATURES

tick-see-day-day weety weety weety

Song Wheezy and accented dropping in pitch at the end.
Behavior Very active; moves in groups, skulks in thickets.
Habitat Oak, juniper and pine woodlands and scrub.

Nest A hole nester including fence posts.
Food Small insects, seeds and berries; at feeder takes peanut butter and sunflower seeds.

hiding owl materialize and dart back with wings a blur. Then it is a half-hour of constant harrying as they call and scold before wandering off in a ragtag group foraging through the woodlands.

A gray bird with a small crest, the plain titmouse lacks the black on the throat of most chickadees, but its harsh chick-a-dee-dee *call is typical. It lives in mixed and deciduous woodlands where it prefers oaks and junipers. Length 5¼ inches*

RED-BREASTED NUTHATCH *Sitta canadensis*

MANY BIRDS ARE NAMED after what they do. Creepers creep, humming birds hum, jays call jay and nuthatches hatch nuts (hatch not meaning incubating but rather open, and nuts alluding to all seed types.) At this job they are quite adept. Not being a very large bird many seeds and fruit types can be formidable tasks to open. In most cases the seed is carried off, wedged into a crevice and pounded on until it is "hatched."

This diminutive bird's actions are very similar to its white-breasted cousin but it prefers coniferous forests to mixed deciduous woodlands. Within these evergreen woods they are bundles of energy working over every trunk and limb, searching every crevice and open cone. Egg masses, larvae, seeds and spiders along with small insects – all are taken. Very often they hang from a branch tip during their investigations – a position their larger relative doesn't get into. They are handsome birds with a blue gray back and rusty underparts and flanks. A bold white line runs over the eye and through the black cap, which extends below the eye.

The common call is a high-pitched nasal *yank*. Upon finding a predator, such as an owl, in the forest bedlam erupts and soon small parties of titmice and chickadees join in the excitement of the find. This species is also an irruptive migrant. On wintering grounds in some years there is a great paucity of the species and then years follow when the evergreen woods are full of them. Like other irruptive species this can lead to nesting in areas such as marsh edges and backyards where they normally would only visit. Nesting is in a natural cavity or hole excavated by the birds. These can be in either deciduous or evergreen trees. If in an evergreen, the area around the entrance hole is smeared with a ring of resin. In many instances this resin acts as an irritant to tree-climbing snakes making them quickly drop off the tree. The birds will also take to nest boxes. These should be placed as close to a prime habitat as possible because the birds are not as adaptive to interacting with man as the white-breasted nuthatch. They come readily to feeding areas during the winter months taking suet and sunflower seeds with great relish.

FACTS AND FEATURES

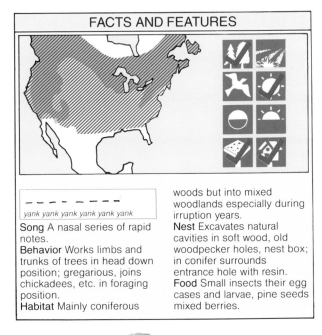

yank yank yank yank yank yank

Song A nasal series of rapid notes.
Behavior Works limbs and trunks of trees in head down position; gregarious, joins chickadees, etc. in foraging position.
Habitat Mainly coniferous woods but into mixed woodlands especially during irruption years.
Nest Excavates natural cavities in soft wood, old woodpecker holes, nest box; in conifer surrounds entrance hole with resin.
Food Small insects their egg cases and larvae, pine seeds mixed berries.

A small active bird with a black cap, distinct white eye line, a black line through the eye and rusty underparts, the red-breasted nuthatch summers in coniferous woodlands, but it rests in other areas during migration and sometimes stays on to nest. Migration is irregular and depends on the supply of conifer seeds. Length 4½ inches

WHITE-BREASTED NUTHATCH *Sitta carolinensis*

A NASAL CALL *yank–yank–yank* is sure to attract attention and the beginning birder who locates the bird has the surprise of seeing a bird walking head-first down a tree! Such diagnostic behavior makes it easy to locate in birdbooks and to log it in as a bird easy to remember. And a handsome bird it is too. With sharp crisp lines the pure white underparts are sharply defined by the jet black cap in the male (gray in the female) and blue-gray back. The flanks are a rusty red. If one looks closely at the bill it can be seen to taper to a chisel point. It is the use of this bill to hatch or open nuts and other seeds that has given this bird its name. To open seeds it will hold them with its feet or more often take them to a rough surface such as tree bark, wedge the seeds in and then hammer them open. If you have a feeder in your yard it is not uncommon to hear pounding on the side of your house early in the morning as a bird jams the seeds in between shingles and then pounds them to split the hard coat. When a good food source is found such as a full feeding station, caching food is another habit. Sunflower seed after sunflower seed will be taken away and stored.

The nest is a natural cavity in a broken limb or tree trunk or perhaps an old woodpecker hole. If the wood is soft enough they will excavate their own hole. Bird boxes are also readily accepted and will be used in the winter as a night roosting area.

A close relative of chickadees and titmice, the nuthatch will often travel with them in foraging flocks especially in the spring, fall and through the winter. When one hears the calls of the chickadee, very often the Nuthatch can be seen scouring trunks and tree limbs. This is a nice feeding and gleaning combination.

Though the call is best known, the song is along the same lines, a series of nasal whistles given on a non-melodic uniform pitch. Although close in sound to the calls, the rapidity of the song is a separating factor. In addition, during its delivery the bird bobs and twists, flutters its wings and cocks its tail as it weaves around a limb in a nuptial display.

Like all nuthatches, this bird travels headfirst down a tree, finding insects missed by other birds that make their way up. It will also eat berries and seeds and is a frequent visitor to birdfeeders. It prefers wooded areas but has adapted well to city and suburban environments. Length 5½ inches

FACTS AND FEATURES

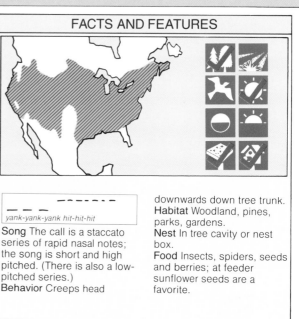

yank-yank-yank hit-hit-hit

Song The call is a staccato series of rapid nasal notes; the song is short and high pitched. (There is also a low-pitched series.)
Behavior Creeps head downwards down tree trunk.
Habitat Woodland, pines, parks, gardens.
Nest In tree cavity or nest box.
Food Insects, spiders, seeds and berries; at feeder sunflower seeds are a favorite.

♀

♂

BROWN CREEPER *Certhia familiaris*

The brown creeper's streaky brown plumage disappears into the woodland background as the bird works its way up tree trunks in a spiral searching for insects, their egg cases or larvae. It sings a musical trill as it darts from one spot to another using its tail as a prop while it searches for food. Length 5 inches

WHILE WALKING UPLAND WOODLANDS the beginning birder may be drawn by a high-pitched *seeeet* note and his eye attracted to what seems like a piece of bark or lichen moving up the trunk of a tree! As the bird pauses to glean an egg case or insect larvae from a fissure in the bark its actual form can be made out – slim with brown and buff streaks, extremely well camouflaged for creeping up trees. The bill is fairly long and curved, just right for probing into cracks and crevices. The feet are unseen because the bird hugs the bark so tightly, and the tail, a rusty color, is sharp-tipped and used as an effective prop as the bird works its way up a trunk to obtain a prey item.

The Brown Creeper is enjoyable to watch in all of its habits. It spirals up a tree, seemingly in quick short "jumps" and upon reaching the uppermost area of investigation simply drops off one tree and flits to the base of another to start a new upward journey. In courtship it has a wonderful, descending musical jumble of notes. After emitting the song it will do a display flight involving rapid flying around the trunk of a tree and spiralling upward. Upon completion of the flight it again calls *seet–tweedlee–deet*. This is a familiar sound in the evergreen woods and wooded swamplands where it nests.

The nest is also memorable – if it can be found – wedged between a loose, hanging bark flap of a dead tree trunk and made of sticks and grasses. It is a wonder that even the slightest breeze does not spill the contents out. The adults visiting the nest approach with the normal hunting appearance as they spiral up the tree and then at the last moment slip from sight. This is a species that is a joy to watch because of its interesting feeding and breeding behavior.

FACTS AND FEATURES

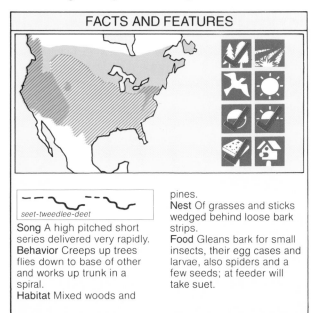

seet-tweedlee-deet

Song A high pitched short series delivered very rapidly.
Behavior Creeps up trees flies down to base of other and works up trunk in a spiral.
Habitat Mixed woods and pines.
Nest Of grasses and sticks wedged behind loose bark strips.
Food Gleans bark for small insects, their egg cases and larvae, also spiders and a few seeds; at feeder will take suet.

CANYON WREN *Catherpes mexicanus*

FACTS AND FEATURES

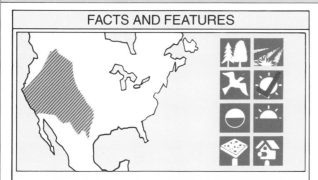

tee — too tew tew too tew

Song A loud ringing series of liquid notes which spiral downwards.
Behavior Creeps about mouse like on rock faces. Will peer at an intruder then quickly disappear.

Habitat Steep-sided canyon faces and rock slides.
Nest Bulky mass of sticks lined with hair or fur, wedged into a rock crevice.
Food All forms of insects, spiders.

STANDING AT THE BASE of canyon walls that seem to rise so high as to narrow the opening at the top to a mere slit of blue sky, the echoing song of the wren seems ethereal. The late ornithologist Ralph Hoffmann colorfully describes the song: "From the bare grim walls of rock the Canyon Wren pours out a cascade of sweet liquid notes, like the spray of a waterfall in sunshine." The cascade is liquid indeed, and consists of a series of rapid downwardly spiralling notes that slow in speed towards the ending: *tee – too, tew, tee – too – tee*.

Finding this songster can be a daunting task. It scampers in and out of cracks and crevices like a mouse. Even when it stops to peer down at an intruder, all that is usually seen is a head quickly popping over a rock edge, and as quickly gone. When finally viewed in the open, creeping up a rock face as it probes for insects, eggs and larvae, the rich chestnut of the back shows in striking contrast to the pure white throat. Finding a morsel, it drops from the face as if shot and disappears into the pile of rocky rubble at the base. The walls and roofs of cabins set within these canyons, are also eagerly investigated in the quest for spiders and small insects.

The nest of twigs, stems and leaves is wedged into a crevice of the rock face and is often very difficult to find or reach. It is only when one finds a site tucked in a wood pile or the like, near human habitation, that one really gets to know the nest of this canyon recluse.

Frequently sighted in canyons and on cliffs, the canyon wren is easily identified by its white throat and breast and its chestnut belly. Its bill is long and thin, its tail rust crossed by black bars and its head, back, wings and abdomen barred and spotted with black and white. Length 5½ inches

CACTUS WREN *Campylorhynchus brunneicapillus*

FACTS AND FEATURES

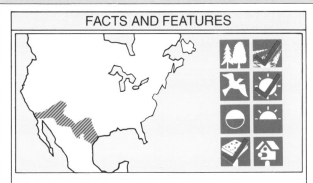

cha cha cha rach chick ra ra

Song Scolding series of harsh notes rising and falling in sequence.
Behavior A skulker, but sings from conspicuous position; attracted by "squeaking".

Habitat Dry areas with cacti.
Nest Globular mass of grasses and twigs with side entrance, sited in a cactus.
Food Insects, cacti fruit, at feeder attracted by fruits such as half oranges.

ARID SCRUB AND CACTUS COUNTRY is the home of this large and attractive wren. So large that many people cannot believe, when they first see it, a wren that is nearly 9in long. As it hops up through the cactus blades and assumes its posture at its singing perch it takes on the familiar erect posture with drooping tail of many of the wrens. Head thrown back and entire body shaking, it pours forth a barrage of *cha–cha–cha–cha–cha* notes interspersed with a few harsh warbling notes. Upon completion the Cactus Wren usually slips back into the thicket and its presence is known only from an occasional harsh scolding *ka–ka–ka*. It sings all day and throughout the year.

The nest is a globular mass of sticks with a side opening and is often placed in its favorite, very spiny, cholla cactus, or one of the prickly pears. In one cactus clump there may be many such nests; one to be used for nesting, others as roosting sites. These cacti areas are often frequented by snakes, and battles between many Cactus Wrens and intruding snakes in search of eggs and young birds can cause a massive uproar in an often serene desert setting.

During the year, especially after the nesting and raising of young is over, the birds will move in closer to civilization. They will visit feeders and one favorite object is half of an orange stuck on a post. The birds will sit by the hour plunging their long curved bill into the fruit allowing the viewer plenty of time to study their rich brown, tawny and boldly streaked body patterns.

By far the biggest wren, the cactus wren lives in thorny scrub and cactus country. Its size as well as its broad white eye stripes, heavily spotted breast and barred wings and tail make it fairly easy to identify. Its longer bill and the white on its back distinguish it from the sage thrasher. Length 8½ inches

BEWICK'S WREN *Thryomanes bewickii*

A bird with a variable, trilling song, Bewick's wren has a brown back, white underparts and a long tail fringed with white which it flicks sideways. Length 5¼ inches

ONE INTERESTING ASPECT of studying birds is determining why certain species are found where. It is obvious that birds that occupy the same niche or lifestyle cannot effectively co-exist in the same area. Yet, in Bewick's Wren we have a bird that appears to lead a double life, depending on the area studied. In the West it is common, interacting with the less common house wren, and appears to be filling the role of the Carolina wren of the East. It prefers the dry chaparral thickets that the house wren seems to disdain, and so in such areas there is no conflict. In areas where the Carolina is dominant, the house wren is basically missing and Bewick's takes on the house wren niche. And in areas where all three are present, the Bewick's appears to be losing ground and withdrawing its range to more stable areas.

In appearance, it looks closest to a Carolina: a rich chestnut back, bold white line over the eye, and gray underparts. It is a species of the waste thicket, brushland, woodland edge and garden thicket and has typical wren actions; very quick, tail cocked high, and a persistent singer. The song is a series of clear introductory notes that seem to be delivered as if inhaled and then exploded, followed by a falling series of trills.

The nest is a natural cavity or abandoned woodpecker excavation. If such a hollow is not available they will wedge the nest of bulky twigs and plant material in rubble piles and rock crevices. They will also make use of bird boxes.

FACTS AND FEATURES

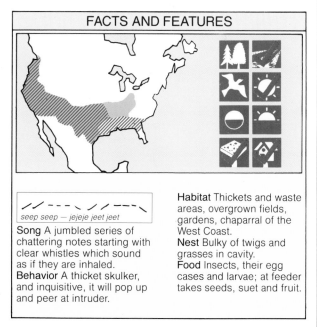

seep seep — jejeje jeet jeet

Song A jumbled series of chattering notes starting with clear whistles which sound as if they are inhaled.
Behavior A thicket skulker, and inquisitive, it will pop up and peer at intruder.

Habitat Thickets and waste areas, overgrown fields, gardens, chaparral of the West Coast.
Nest Bulky of twigs and grasses in cavity.
Food Insects, their egg cases and larvae; at feeder takes seeds, suet and fruit.

HOUSE WREN *Troglodytes aedon*

FEW BIRDS HAVE ADAPTED better to alterations of habitat than the House Wren, which has taken advantage of man-made structures and waste. Birdhouses are readily accepted for a home but so is the eave corner of a garage or old shed. Brush piles are scoured by the adults for insect food. No disturbance within reason seems to perplex this mighty mite of the bird world. Always in action, one may pop up at any time in its pursuit of food for the young.

The nest is a bulky structure of coarse sticks collected anew or re-used after being meticulously removed from a nest box by the returning male. Even though it is the same nest used the previous year it will be removed and then rebuilt. If there are several nest boxes available don't be surprised to see all of them stuffed with sticks by a pair of wrens. Some are dummy nests to fool predators looking for the one with eggs and one may be used as the night roost box by the male. To thwart competition for food within its territory by other species the House Wren also has the unlikable habit of piercing other birds' eggs with its longish bill.

Its song is an explosion of sound. Roller-coasting up and down, the jumble of gurgling and bubbly notes seems to pour out and roll on and on. Over and over the song is repeated throughout the day. Not only does this species sing from its favorite perch but also from the top of the nesting box after delivering food, from the branches of trees and bushes while searching for food and from just about any place it stops during its daily activities. When the wren is in the yard its song will always tell you where it is. After the nesting season it falls silent and then assumes rather secretive ways and can be difficult to get a good view.

As with all members of the wren family the basic coloration is brown. It is paler below than above with obscure flanks bars. There is a pale line over the eye. The tail is often cocked on an angle but when working in the thicket is held straight out.

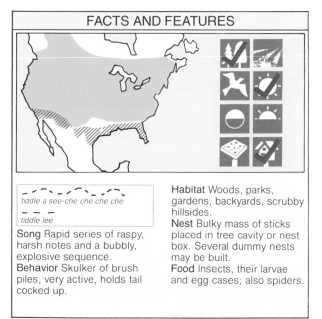

FACTS AND FEATURES

tiddle a see-che che che che

tiddle lee

Song Rapid series of raspy, harsh notes and a bubbly, explosive sequence.
Behavior Skulker of brush piles, very active, holds tail cocked up.

Habitat Woods, parks, gardens, backyards, scrubby hillsides.
Nest Bulky mass of sticks placed in tree cavity or nest box. Several dummy nests may be built.
Food Insects, their larvae and egg cases; also spiders.

A house wren at the threshold of its nest hole in an old tree stump. House wrens are easily attracted to nest boxes in the garden. Where they are common in the area, at least two boxes should be put up because wrens more than most other birds like to build dummy nests. Make a slot for the entrance rather than a hole as this allows the birds to maneuver longer twigs. Wren boxes should be about 7 inches high with an inside measurement of 4×4 inches square.

This energetic summer visitor differs from other wrens in its lack of obvious head markings and from the winter wren in its plain breast, longer tail and larger size. In a characteristic movement, it cocks its tail over its back. Length 4½ inches

WINTER WREN *Troglodytes troglodytes*

THIS TINY MITE of a bird often slips by unnoticed, especially during migration when it travels from the northern extremes of its range to its southern limits. It tends to be shy and its size (4in) makes it difficult to locate even when the birder knows it is creeping about in a nearby thicket. More often than not, the sharp *chip – ship* note in rapid sequence gives its presence away. Skulking around near or on the ground it may pop into view for a moment, make brief scolding noises, then slip back into the dense thickets. Deep brown in color with heavy barring on the flanks, it cocks its tail up in typical wren manner. During the breeding season its preferred habitat is the cool, damp coniferous forests of the North and West. The sweet, twittering endless song of this small bird is heard to best advantage here, along a cold rushing mountain stream. Its continuous outpouring seems to last beyond the limits of so very small a songster.

The nest – a domed structure of rootlets, fibers and moss – is placed on the ground, under an overhanging edge, rocky concavity or in a dense brushy area. Several nests are made and scattered throughout its territory: being polygamous, the male replaces each brood in rapid succession with another female.

For the majority of American birders the name "Winter Wren" holds true as it is most often seen on migration or during the winter months. It uses a wide range of habitats, but is always around a dense thicket or brush pile.

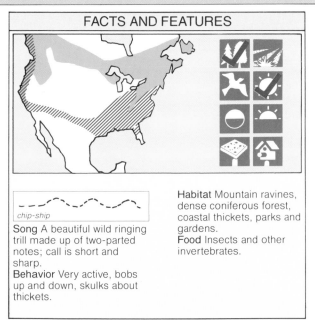

FACTS AND FEATURES

chip-ship

Song A beautiful wild ringing trill made up of two-parted notes; call is short and sharp.
Behavior Very active, bobs up and down, skulks about thickets.

Habitat Mountain ravines, dense coniferous forest, coastal thickets, parks and gardens.
Food Insects and other invertebrates.

A permanent population of this bird exists in the west of its range, from Southern California north along the coast out onto the most distant island of the Aleutian Chain, Attu. There the species reaches its maximum size – nearly that of a house wren! This wren is also found throughout Europe.

The smallest of the wrens, this bird has a short stubby tail, which it cocks up, and dark bars on its belly. It also has an unusual bobbing movement. The winter wren lives in thick undergrowth in woods and is secretive and hard to spot. Length 4 inches

MARSH WREN *Cistothorus palustris*

IF PURE ENERGY were packaged in feathers a prime candidate would be the Marsh Wren. A visit to any cattail or reed marsh in either a fresh or brackish situation will confirm this. Sitting quietly at the edge of such an area the loud rapid jumbled notes of the singing males will be heard from all sectors. Even the song seems hurried. Small tawny brown forms will be seen hurtling over the cattails then plunging from sight. To see one in close, make a squeaking sound on the back of your hand and wait. Soon a scolding *sh–sh–sh–sh* will be heard followed by *check, check, check*. At last the wren will come into view, usually hanging spread-legged between two cattail stalks. Tiny in body, the strong white line over the eye accentuates its staring inquisitiveness. The back is a streaked rust color with white below running into buff on the flanks. It remains interested only until it is satisfied that the intruder does not pose a threat, then it is quickly gone.

Working one's way deep into the reeds the energies of this bird's nesting habits can also be appreciated. There are football-shaped nests seemingly everywhere. One characteristic of wrens is dummy nesting. In the Marsh Wren it is expressed to the maximum. One bird may build 15 nests on its territory; one for nesting, usually the most difficult to locate, and the others acting as decoys for predators and therefore in much more obvious positions. These may also be used as roosting sites by the male. They are woven from leaves and fibers of sedges and cattails and have a side entrance. The energy expended for such a nest grouping must be incredible.

Food consists of all forms of small insects and even invertebrates taken on the mud surfaces or left exposed on previously submerged plant stalks. The activity carries on through the night as singing will go non-stop on through the nesting season. Fledglings move about in little groups following the parents across ditches and among the reeds begging for food. At this time the marsh seems to be alive with brown dots that look like insect infestations rather than birds. As the marsh begins to freeze in late fall most birds head south, but some linger on in the North and manage to find the energy to even sing on the coldest of mornings. Energy and wrens just seem to go hand in hand.

Its larger size, solid rust brown cap and the white above the eye and on the underparts help distinguish this bird from the short-billed marsh wren. It prefers to live in cattail swamps and reedy marshes. Length 5 inches·

FACTS AND FEATURES

sh-sh-sh

Song A bubbling series of harsh notes delivered in a rapid rolling pattern; call *sh-sh-sh* or *check-check*.
Behavior Climbs nimbly about reeds, sings from reed stalk; flies with stiff wings.

Habitat Fresh and brackish reed and cattail marshes.
Nest A football-shaped mass of plant fibers with side entry hole. Builds dummy nests to fool predators.
Food Small insects and invertebrates, seeds on occasion.

DIPPER *Cinclus mexicanus*

ALONG THE CLEAR RUSHING TORRENTS OF mountain streams of the western United States the birder will often catch sight of a uniform gray ball-like bird "buzzing" up- or down-stream on fast beating wings. As it passes a sharp alarm call *beezeeep* can be heard. The bird is the Dipper or Water Ouzel, the term Ouzel coming from the Old English name for blackbird.

When heard for the first time it is hard to believe that the song is being produced by such a bulky little bird. It is a beautiful, strong song made up of trills and flute like notes more like that of a thrush or wren rather than a Dipper.

If persistent the birder can often find the Dipper working the rocks along the river's edge and this is when it is seen to best advantage. As it bobs along from rock to rock it is constantly looking for invertebrates. Stout-bodied with short tail the gray of the body runs into a dull brownish tint to the head and neck. This is best seen in bright sunlight, otherwise the bird looks a uniform gray. As it blinks, white eyelids can be seen. Finding a shallow edge to its liking it walks directly in and slowly disappears from sight. Observing such a pool from above the bird can be seen actively working its way along the pool bottom. Literally walking underwater! If it encounters turbulent water the wings come into play and it gives the feeling of flying beneath the surface. Upon securing food it bobs to the surface and quickly takes flight to the nest site.

The nest is a beautiful structure and with patience can be located. Usually placed in the spray at the edge or even under a waterfall overhang or in the dripping

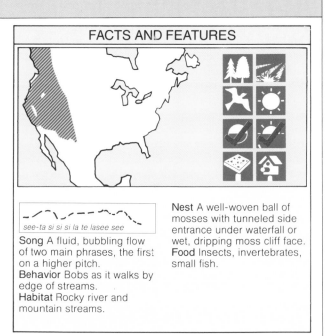

FACTS AND FEATURES

see-ta si si si la te lasee see

Song A fluid, bubbling flow of two main phrases, the first on a higher pitch.
Behavior Bobs as it walks by edge of streams.
Habitat Rocky river and mountain streams.

Nest A well-woven ball of mosses with tunneled side entrance under waterfall or wet, dripping moss cliff face.
Food Insects, invertebrates, small fish.

edges of moss-covered cliffs over the river it blends remarkably well with the surroundings. More often than not it is discovered when the adult returns to the rocks below it, looks about and then flies up to disappear before one's eyes into the mossy bank! Close inspection with binoculars will reveal a tight ball-like nest made of mosses. As the young grow the bird returning to the nest will be met at the door by four gaping yellow mouths looking for food. To this end the bird often cannot even land but quickly jams food into the nearest mouth and drops back down onto the river's edge.

Dippers seem to love to sing and even through the winter where streams stay open the songs can be heard cascading down the riverine canyons along with the rush of the frigid waters. It is truly a bird of the North American wild, rather sedentary in existence. The only migration made is down from the high country to open water below where it will winter, awaiting its return to the waterfalls and wildflowers in spring.

The dipper gets its name from its habit of bobbing its body up and down by bending its legs. It lives along mountain streams and swims, dives and even walks underwater. Its song is similar to a wren's. Length 7½ inches·

Ruby-crowned Kinglet *Regulus calendula*

Ji–jit–ji–jit is a common sound in thickets during spring and fall migration across the continent. The caller is the Ruby-crowned Kinglet, one of the smallest North American birds. Hardly ever at a standstill it flicks about in the bushes and has the constant habit of twitching its wings. Nervously moving about it will often move in very close to the birder before working off through the thickets again. It is a grayish-olive bird with a distinct broken eye ring of white and strong white wingbars. The young fall birds have yellowish wingbars.

As for the ruby cap, don't expect to see it very often. Only when in courtship display (which involves flitting about with feathers raised, wings spread and tail cocked) or when angry at a predator do the birds raise their vermillion central crown feathers into view. But once flared out it is a sight not easily forgotten.

Nor is the full song of the bird one that is difficult to forget. It is hard to believe that this mite of a bird has such a loud ringing song, an explosion – *see–see–see teedle teedle teedle*. Early in spring it is on its way to the evergreen northern forests, mountain glens of the West and willow hillsides of the far North.

The nest is a beautiful cup of plant fibers, lined with plant down and covered with lichens and spiderweb. The inside is lined with a deep layer of feathers. This

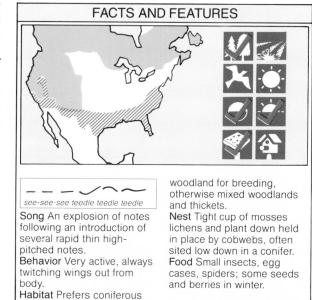

FACTS AND FEATURES

see-see-see teedle teedle teedle

Song An explosion of notes following an introduction of several rapid thin high-pitched notes.
Behavior Very active, always twitching wings out from body.
Habitat Prefers coniferous woodland for breeding, otherwise mixed woodlands and thickets.
Nest Tight cup of mosses lichens and plant down held in place by cobwebs, often sited low down in a conifer.
Food Small insects, egg cases, spiders; some seeds and berries in winter.

species represents a group of immigrant birds known as the Old World warblers and have more direct ties with the thrushes than our native wood warblers.

A small bird with the habit of flicking its wings, the ruby-crowned kinglet is common in woodlands with dense undergrowth where it eats insects and spiders. The male has brilliant red brown feathers which it holds erect in display or when it is agitated. Length 4½ inches

BLUE-GRAY GNATCATCHER *Polioptila caerulea*

YOUR ATTENTION will probably first be drawn to the bird because of the thin, explosive *spit–tseee* it utters while working in a thicket or upper limbs of a tree. When seen, more often than not, it will be working its way out along a branch with tail flicking side to side as it hops about. Its base color is a subtle blue-gray. The tail is very thin and long and edged with white contrasting to the black central portion. The white eye ring seems to accentuate the beady black eye. Some know the species as the "miniature mockingbird." Not only is the color pattern the same but when it breaks into song it is loud, rollicking and effervescent. How can such a small bird produce such a loud song?

Its favorite haunts are woodlands and thickets and in the West is found right down to the coastal scrub. The beautiful nest is constructed on the open ribs of trees. Made of woven plant fibers and down, the outside is decorated with lichens. The birds when building will make innumerable trips to pick off small swatches of gray and green lichens then anchor them to the walls of the nest using cobwebs. During the nesting season it is not uncommon to see these birds fluttering in between branches seemingly attacking nothing. More often than not they are actually fluttering up for cobweb silk. The young are tiny gray tufts of feathers that bounce along behind the adults begging food and quickly gobbling down larvae, eggs and other insect material that is collected from the bark crevices by the adults. The adults will often pursue insects in flight in the upper tree branches twisting and turning with the audible clicking of the bill.

This long-tailed bundle of energy is a mite of a bird

FACTS AND FEATURES

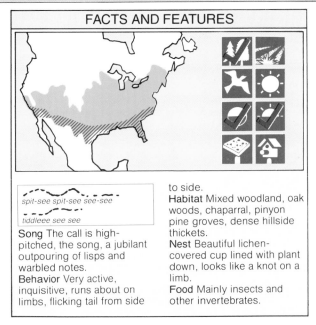

spit-see spit-see see-see

tiddleee see see

Song The call is high-pitched, the song, a jubilant outpouring of lisps and warbled notes.
Behavior Very active, inquisitive, runs about on limbs, flicking tail from side to side.
Habitat Mixed woodland, oak woods, chaparral, pinyon pine groves, dense hillside thickets.
Nest Beautiful lichen-covered cup lined with plant down, looks like a knot on a limb.
Food Mainly insects and other invertebrates.

and is becoming more and more widespread to the north of its former range. At one time considered to be a southern species the range has inched its way slowly northward to its present limitation in eastern Canada.

On the wintering grounds in areas such as Florida and Texas this species can be abundant. Though they seldom sing their loud bubbling song during the winter months the loud *spit–cheeee* is given and allows one to realize how common this species is in these semi-tropical forests.

An active bird that swings its long tail as it hops along a tree branch, the blue-gray gnatcatcher lives high up in trees in woodland areas and flycatches for insects and spiders. It has a loud whistling song with wheezing notes. Length 4½ inches

♀

♂

EASTERN BLUEBIRD *Sialia sialis*

♀

♂

A thrush with blue upperparts contrasting with rich rust below and a white underbelly, the bluebird is one of the best known songbirds in the US. It perches high up in trees and drops down to seize insects, then returning to its perch. It also eats fruits, berries and seeds. Length 7 inches

SELDOM HAS A BIRD ENDEARED itself to so many. Certainly the sight of one flying up from beside the road and perching on a fencepost is a sight that excites even the non-birder. The spectacular blue contrasting with the orange and white of the underparts is a most striking combination. The song is a short soft warble often repeated.

The sighting of bluebirds is often the talk of the day from garden plot to farmyard and most people are aware that they do not see as many bluebirds as they did in the past. Several things have affected the Bluebird's nesting success. The introduction of the European starling certainly is a main factor. Eviction from nesting holes, be they man-made or natural, is commonplace. In addition, the species has very specific needs for a nest site, favorite sites being old trees with holes, lining pastureland. But a great deal of the East has lost such pastureland and with it, the bluebird population. The birds can however be encouraged with bird boxes set on posts fairly low to the ground near a woodland edge but in a position that is open on all sides. Unfortunately such a site is also attractive to tree swallows which often usurp the nest box. To counter this sabotage, "Bluebird Trails" have been established where large numbers of boxes are placed at intervals in ideal habitats, affording a wide selection for nesting. And therein lies the hope of the future for

this lovely bird, and indeed in many areas such as the Midwest and Southern Canada, the Bluebird is making a remarkable comeback. More "pieces of azure" to delight generations to come.

FACTS AND FEATURES

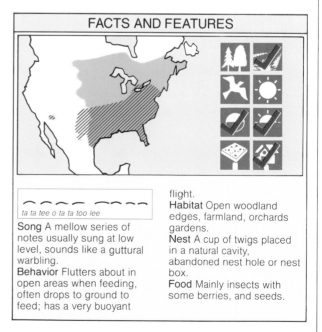

ta ta tee o ta ta too lee

Song A mellow series of notes usually sung at low level, sounds like a guttural warbling.
Behavior Flutters about in open areas when feeding, often drops to ground to feed; has a very buoyant flight.
Habitat Open woodland edges, farmland, orchards gardens.
Nest A cup of twigs placed in a natural cavity, abandoned nest hole or nest box.
Food Mainly insects with some berries, and seeds.

MOUNTAIN BLUEBIRD *Sialia currucoides*

AT THE EDGES OF rolling mountain meadows clothed in wild flowers or on the high gray-green sagebrush plains dwells this bird of startling sky-blue color. In fact the male Mountain Bluebird is entirely blue of various shades. This coloration alone makes it very easy to identify but in addition it has a most peculiar feeding method. From high meadow to timberline, it forages for insects among low shrubs by hovering next to the branches and gleaning food items from limbs and leaves. With rapidly beating wings it swings about the plant and upon grabbing an insect will alight on the ground to eat it or flutter off on bouyant wingbeats to a nearby limb to feed. When first seen this feeding behavior puzzles the birder. It appears that someone is pulling a string, marionette-like, to keep the bird suspended and moving about the bushes.

The song is much like that of the other bluebirds. A soft warble but with a harsher raspy ending. More often a soft *weer* note is heard as one approaches their territory.

The nesting site is a natural tree cavity or old woodpecker hole, often in aspen and birch trees. To see a pair of these bluebirds actively tending a nest in the brilliant white bark of a birch is an unforgettable sight.

When winter comes to the high country the popula-

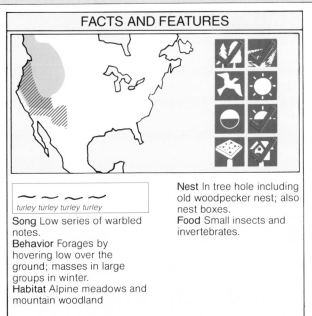

FACTS AND FEATURES

turley turley turley turley

Song Low series of warbled notes.
Behavior Forages by hovering low over the ground; masses in large groups in winter.
Habitat Alpine meadows and mountain woodland

Nest In tree hole including old woodpecker nest; also nest boxes.
Food Small insects and invertebrates.

tion shifts to the rolling plains and extensive agricultural areas to the south, where a winter flock can provide the birder with a sight they will long remember.

As its name implies, the mountain bluebird lives at altitudes of 5,000 feet or more. It prefers farmland and the edges of woodlands where it hovers above the ground seeking insects. It lacks the eastern bluebird's reddish brown breast. Length 7¼ inches·

VEERY *Catharus fuscescens*

WITHIN THE EMERALD CONFINES of the moist mixed woods of the northern United States and southern Canada, a haunting flute-like song cascades down the scale. The songster is the Veery, a shy, reddish-brown thrush with faint chest spotting. To get to know this bird one must venture into the moist woodlands and spend some time sitting and watching. It is not uncommon when one is perfectly still to see this thrush hopping about as it actively feeds among the leaves and mosses. At these times it will approach quite closely and if you are lucky it may fly up to a low limb, toss back its head and pour forth that wonderful song.

Once heard or sited, if one explores a Veery's habitat, you may be fortunate to find the cup nest of bark, grass and rootlets. This is often placed on the ground but may also be tucked into the base of a shrub. The coloration of the eggs is a beautiful pastel blue and when seen within the dark wet woodlands they appear to glow like embers from the nest.

As with all the thrushes the joy of hearing their songs from the depths of the woodlands on a spring evening is a pleasure that is hard to match in the birding world.

Note: The eastern birder has to be aware that when in the same habitat in the West the songster may look somewhat different. A darker brown in color with more distinct spotting, it looks quite similar to its close relative, the Swainson's thrush. However, the Veery lacks the large conspicuous eye ring and pale sides of the Swainson's.

FACTS AND FEATURES

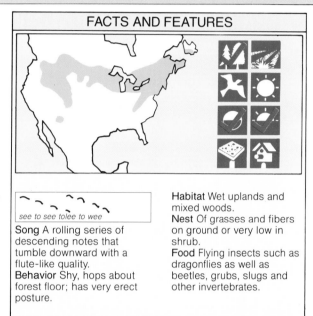

see to see tolee to wee

Song A rolling series of descending notes that tumble downward with a flute-like quality.
Behavior Shy, hops about forest floor; has very erect posture.

Habitat Wet uplands and mixed woods.
Nest Of grasses and fibers on ground or very low in shrub.
Food Flying insects such as dragonflies as well as beetles, grubs, slugs and other invertebrates.

A summer resident in dense forests, wet areas and mixed woodlands in the northern states, the veery runs along the ground in short bursts stopping to look for insects. It is a tame bird with a down-spiraling flute-like song. Length 7 inches

SWAINSON'S THRUSH *Catharus ustulatus*

FACTS AND FEATURES

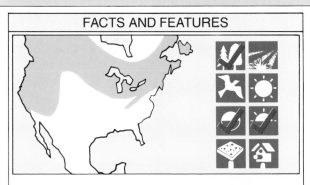

tee-twaoo-tee ee ta lee

Song A series of ascending whistles.
Behavior Often droops and twitches its wings; fairly shy — spends most of its time feeding on the ground but sings from treetop.

Habitat Cool northern forests otherwise mixed woods on migration.
Nest Cup of grasses and plant fibers most often just above ground in shrub.
Food Wide variety of small insects, larvae, seeds, and berries.

ALL THE NORTHERN FOREST thrushes seem to have the same basic color pattern, and this species is no exception. The rich olive to brownish color of the back is quite variable, and there is smudged spotting on the buff-tinted breast. Perhaps the best identifying mark lies in the wide buff-colored eyering, and in its habit of twitching its wings.

Swainson's Thrush is a bird of swamplands and moist woodland floors and in migration can be quite abundant. Indeed, on clear fall nights when the first cool winds cascade down from the North, hundreds of these birds migrating overhead in the blackness of night can be heard giving their diagnostic *qweep* calls. A visit to the woodlands the next morning may result in seeing several feeding on insects, berries and seeds as they fatten up to continue their journey.

The song is whistled without the true flute-like quality of a wood thrush and is delivered in an ascending scale. It is usually sung from a low perch because the bird prefers to be close to the ground. When nesting, however, it breaks this rule, and I have occasionally seen the cup nest of twigs, leaves, bark strips and lichens set as high as 20ft up in a conifer. More often, it is placed a couple of feet off the ground in a scraggy shrub.

Birds that forage on the ground come into contact with a myriad of insects, mites and the like, and this species seems to be prone to carrying ticks on fleshy parts near the eye, mouth edge and in ear openings. Extensive studies are underway to ascertain if this bird is a possible vector for arboviruses and, if so, it could explain their rapid spread at times.

This bird can be distinguished from other thrushes by its light tan face and eye ring. It lacks the red on the tail that the hermit thrush has, and its breast is more heavily spotted than the veery's. It is fairly common in coniferous forests and thickets of alder and willow trees, but it is shy and retiring. Length 7 inches

HERMIT THRUSH *Catharus guttatus*

THE SWAMP ANGEL! Names such as this illustrate how beautiful this bird's song really is. A series of flute-like echoing-notes that seem to drift in the air for seconds after the song is delivered. All thrushes tend to have beautiful voices but this species is often voted to have the best.

The Hermit Thrush is a species of coniferous and mixed upland woods. Wet areas and cool ravine thickets are preferred within these habitats and such settings certainly add to the ethereal quality of the song. On the West Coast where the evergreen forests extend down to the shore, this thrush is fairly common but its shyness gives no clue to its abundance. Across Canada it is a widespread nester and on the East Coast it nests in scattered localities of cool bog and swampland. In the South it is a fall migrant and an overwintering species. This is yet another species that seems so out of place in Mexico after getting to know it so well in the cool boreal forests. On the wintering rounds its presence is often given away by a distinct *chuck* note as the bird forages in a dense thicket. If it does hop into view it will be seen raising its tail slowly to a cocked position, slowly lowering it and then flicking it up again. This is an excellent field mark, as is the rusty tail contrasting to the brown back. It also has a conspicuous white eye ring. As with any species that inhabits a wide range of habitats many subspecies occur but the reddish tail

FACTS AND FEATURES

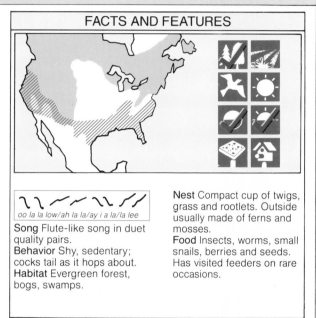

oo la la low/ah la la/ay i a la/la lee

Song Flute-like song in duet quality pairs.
Behavior Shy, sedentary; cocks tail as it hops about.
Habitat Evergreen forest, bogs, swamps.

Nest Compact cup of twigs, grass and rootlets. Outside usually made of ferns and mosses.
Food Insects, worms, small snails, berries and seeds. Has visited feeders on rare occasions.

pattern is a consistent feature.

Getting to know this species on the breeding grounds can lead not only to beautiful localities but also to the treat of hearing one of the best North American songsters.

Considered by many to be the finest songster in North America, the hermit thrush sings with a flute-like sound in ringing two-toned notes. It is a shy bird that spends much of its time on the ground in dense coniferous forests and swampy thickets searching for insects and seeds. In winter, it eats berries. Length 6-6¼ inches

WOOD THRUSH *Hylocichla mustelina*

THE WOOD THRUSH is most at home where the dappled light strikes the forest floor beneath a lush understory. It hops about in typical thrush manner, pausing now and then to look about with an upright posture. Cocking its head, it flicks aside some leaves to seize an insect larva.

It is a richly colored bird, with the bright reddish-brown on the head running off into a warm brown on its back and white underparts heavily marked with dark teardrop spotting. Its habitat preference is wide: from laurel thickets of dryer upland woods to the cool shaded swamplands of the eastern forests, the liquid notes of a rich, flute-like quality are a common summer sound.

This thrush seems to prefer singing during the early morning, or evening hours just prior to sunset. At these times listen for the diagnostic *pip – pip – pip* call note. In most instances this is the introductory phrase delivered before the song. Then comes the outpouring of the full *ee–oh–lay* notes that scale downward. These evening "vespers" will continue until just before dark when again the *pip – pip – pip* notes are delivered in rapid sequence until they taper off and the nights are given over to high-pitched hooting of barred owls that often frequent the same woodland habitats.

The nest, typical of the thrushes, is mud-lined. However, the wood thrush tends to add grass and rootlets to the inside, and the outside – loose in

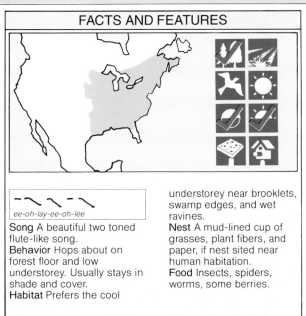

FACTS AND FEATURES

ee-oh-lay-ee-oh-lee

Song A beautiful two toned flute-like song.
Behavior Hops about on forest floor and low understorey. Usually stays in shade and cover.
Habitat Prefers the cool understorey near brooklets, swamp edges, and wet ravines.
Nest A mud-lined cup of grasses, plant fibers, and paper, if nest sited near human habitation.
Food Insects, spiders, worms, some berries.

structure with grass, leaves, vine bark and even paper products (around human habitation) – gives the nest a rather shaggy appearance. It is placed firmly in the crotch of a shrub or small tree.

The wood thrush prefers to live and nest in the lower undergrowth in woodlands and swamps where it finds insects, worms, berries and seeds to eat. It is similar in appearance to the thrasher, but it has a shorter tail, dark eyes and a spotted breast. Length 7¾ inches

ROBIN *Turdus migratorius*

Probably the best-known bird in this country, the robin can often be seen searching for insects or pulling out worms in backyards. Most migrate to the South to escape severe winters; those that stay on eat fruits and berries. Length 10 inches

THIS IS THE BEST-KNOWN of all the songbirds in the United States. Because of its catholic taste in habitat preference it can be found from the deep woodlands to the tiniest park in the largest of cities. During an early morning walk through the building-lined "canyons" in the center of New York City I have heard the fluid notes of the Robin as they poured down from atop a tree in a rooftop garden! It is during the early morning hours and late in the evening as sunset tints the treetops that the song of the Robin is heard to best advantage. Clear flowing notes that see-saw back and forth in their emphasis. Liquid tones that are quickly learned by the birder and awaited by many to signal the end of a harsh northern winter.

The nest of the species is almost as well-known as the bird itself. As the leaves of autumn tumble to the ground the unmasking often reveals a mud-lined cup with grassy outside wedged firmly in the crotch of a tree or bush. Very often the nest was quite close to a well-walked path and has been overlooked while the birds were in occupancy. The eggs are so familiar that everyone is aware of the color of "robin's egg blue."

In the spring when territorial boundaries are being established the Robin can be seen singing from its favorite perches that delineate the area. During this time it is also very defensive of the area and mad chases and tumbling fights often ensue when another male robin crosses its boundary. It is during this defense time that the males will also challenge their own reflections! Battles waged against windows and even hubcaps of cars which reflect will go on for hours.

One of the favorite foods of this species is worms in addition to grubs and insects. Care should be taken concerning lawn preparations to ensure against mass poisonings which have occurred from time to time when individuals or companies have treated a lawn with toxic weedkillers. Check before treating.

During the winter months the food shifts to berries and other fruits. Old apple orchards provide excellent overwintering areas for robins in the North.

FACTS AND FEATURES

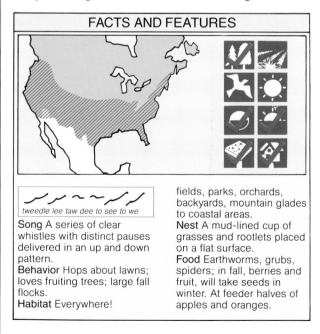

tweedle lee taw dee to see to we

Song A series of clear whistles with distinct pauses delivered in an up and down pattern.
Behavior Hops about lawns; loves fruiting trees; large fall flocks.
Habitat Everywhere!

fields, parks, orchards, backyards, mountain glades to coastal areas.
Nest A mud-lined cup of grasses and rootlets placed on a flat surface.
Food Earthworms, grubs, spiders; in fall, berries and fruit, will take seeds in winter. At feeder halves of apples and oranges.

VARIED THRUSH *Ixoreus naevius*

Orange underparts crossed by a black breast band, an orange line behind the eye and orange brown wing bars and patches make the male of this species easy to identify. The female has a brown breast band and back. The varied thrush lives in damp coniferous woods. Length 9¼ inches

WHEN I FIRST VISITED THE WEST and had the chance to walk through the magnificent cathedral stands of western evergreens, the haunting ethereal notes of the Varied Thrush impressed me as much as any song has. As shafts of gold filtered down on the reddish mat of evergreen needles the songsters hopped into view atop a moss-covered stump. Their body conformation is almost identical to a robin. The back a bluish gray, a bold orange line over the eye and the orange of the underparts shows a chest band of gray, and the wings are marked by orange wing bars which flash brightly when the bird is in flight.

It hopped from the stump, foraged in the needles and ate an insect. It then hopped back up and sang the distinct, nasal penetrating whistle. Slow and drawn out first on one pitch, then a second at a lower pitch followed by a third higher on the scale. A nearby deer broke a twig in its approach, and the thrush was off. In general these birds are quite shy and getting a good view is by chance or long vigilance.

It is a bird of the high mountain forests and the misty evergreen woodlands of the northwest coastline. In Alaska it can also be found in the alder woodlands of streambeds with dense tangles of Devil's club.

In general a bird of the West, recently more and more records of these birds have been noted at winter feeding stations in the East.

FACTS AND FEATURES

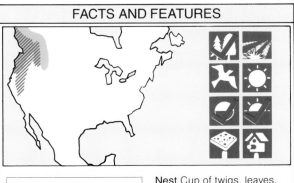

wheeeee wheee wheee wheee

Song A series of drawn out buzzing whistles each delivered on a different pitch.
Behavior Shy, feeds on forest floor, hops in robin fashion.
Habitat Dense coniferous forest.

Nest Cup of twigs, leaves, grasses lined with mud and leaves placed on limb near trunk.
Food Insects and earthworms.

TOWNSEND'S SOLITAIRE *Myadestes townsendi*

THIS THRUSH LIVES in the high, cool, coniferous forests of the West, where mountain torrents wash the bases of steep rocky slopes. I am not sure just how many I have walked past in my days afield, but not many, because they are extremely sedentary birds. Perched on a dead branch usually quite low in the tree, they sit in a bolt-upright position surveying the area. Reluctant to fly except to capture food, they often trustingly allow the birder to pass by at a close distance.

Their plumage is a dull gray, and this somber color affords them the camouflage to allow such bold indulgence. When they fly, however, distinct buffy patches can be seen in the wing, and the outer edge of the tail is

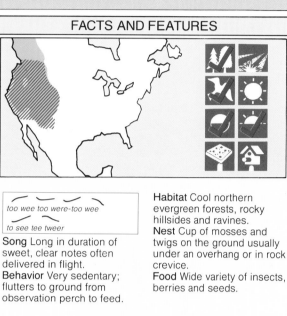

FACTS AND FEATURES

too wee too were-too wee
to see tee tweer

Song Long in duration of sweet, clear notes often delivered in flight.
Behavior Very sedentary; flutters to ground from observation perch to feed.

Habitat Cool northern evergreen forests, rocky hillsides and ravines.
Nest Cup of mosses and twigs on the ground usually under an overhang or in rock crevice.
Food Wide variety of insects, berries and seeds.

white. From their perch on a snag or rocky outcrop they plunge to the ground to snatch up an insect and then return to the roost site much in the manner of hunting bluebirds. The nest is a cup of mosses and twigs and is placed on the ground under a rocky overhang or the base of a shrub or tree.

In the jumbled rocky canyons of interior Alaska I have listened at length as they sang from high on the canyon walls. Grosbeak-like in quality and long in duration (timed for over half a minute) the birds often launch into flight during the song and fly in a circling pattern with wings aflutter. Upon the song's completion the bird spirals down to the initial singing perch.

Young birds are heavily scaled in appearance but have the eyering, buff wing bars and white outer tail feathers of the adult. These thrushes are migratory and in their wanderings may show up from time to time on the East Coast – a long way from home territory.

As this bird swoops off to catch a flying insect, its tan wing patches and white outer tail feathers show. At rest, its brown-gray back and underparts and its white eye ring are its distinguishing features. Length 8½ inches

MOCKINGBIRD *Mimus polyglottos*

ON MOONLIGHT NIGHTS in early May from atop a dense thicket the twisting, wing-fluttering form of the Mockingbird can be seen as it bursts forth with song through the night. One of the few songbirds that sing during the night, the Mockingbird seems to be so filled with song that a full day of singing just doesn't get it all out! As its Latin name implies this is indeed a "many-tongued mimic;" the master mimic of the United States. From a tree top, post, bush top or any convenient position the Mockingbird pours forth its jumble of notes and cries intermixed with mimicked songs of other species. There seems to be no end of their capabilities as the species will mimic the local birds from every sector of the country in which they occur. From killdeer to phoebe, bluebird to jay, no song is too difficult to reproduce. The repertoire acts as an inventory for the species in the area. As new species migrate in for the summer it is not long before their songs are added to the Mocker's outpouring. The renditions are so well-performed at times that they can fool even the most seasoned birder. The function of this mimicking has been a point of contention for a long time. Recent studies have shown that there is a positive effect to keeping birds of other species out of the Mocker's range via this song imitation allowing less pressures on the Mocker's food supply. Rather than being specific in song a wide range is covered to allow maximum effectiveness.

The nest is tucked into the midst of the densest bush which usually provides the main singing perch for the bird on territory. In the East multiflora rose thickets are favored and the spread of the Mockingbird into the

FACTS AND FEATURES

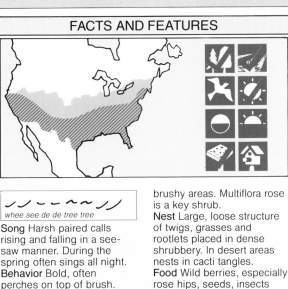

whee see de de tree tree

Song Harsh paired calls rising and falling in a see-saw manner. During the spring often sings all night.
Behavior Bold, often perches on top of brush.
Habitat Gardens, farmlands, parks, backyards. Any

brushy areas. Multiflora rose is a key shrub.
Nest Large, loose structure of twigs, grasses and rootlets placed in dense shrubbery. In desert areas nests in cacti tangles.
Food Wild berries, especially rose hips, seeds, insects and other invertebrates. Rare at feeder.

A mockingbird's light and dark gray plumage (left) helps camouflage it amongst these branches and foliage shadows. Mockingbirds tend to sing from prominent perches.

A mockingbird (above) challenges its own image in a side-view mirror. The mockingbird is generally aggressive and will drive off most other birds from the winter feeder.

A common bird in cities, gardens and open areas, the mockingbird is well known for singing its own song as well as for mimicking other birds. It flushes out insects with wing flashes and tail spreading. In winter it eats the fruits of holly, hackberry, sumac and Virginia creeper. Length 11 inches

Northeast over the last 20-30 years is based on the spread of the rose. On a cold winter's day all one needs to do is drive the back country roads and dotted in the ball-like rose thickets will be the gray form of the Mockingbird.

Undaunted in defense of its territory the Mocker takes on all comers. Many a cat has felt the wrath of a male Mocker as it crossed the bird's territory; with white wing and tail patches flashing, an aerial bombardment occurs that sends fur flying.

A very popular bird, it is the chosen bird of five states. No longer a bird of the Spanish moss-draped trees of southern plantations the Mockingbird has made inroads throughout the country – and into the hearts of many. Its musical outpourings on a bright sunny day are sure to pick up the spirits of anyone who hears it. However, be cautious when asking someone what they think of a Mockingbird's song if they have a resident pair next to their house after a series of bright moonlight nights in May!

GRAY CATBIRD *Dumetella carolinensis*

With its gray color, black cap and mewing sound, the catbird is a familiar summer visitor in the Northeast. It feasts on a wide variety of fruits and berries including blackberries, cherries, elderberries, cat brier berries, mulberries, and blueberries. Those who stay on for the winter eat the fruits of holly, bittersweet and honeysuckle. Length 8½ inches

ORNITHOLOGY STUDENTS always ask, "What is that cat-like mewing coming from the thicket?" This makes it all the easier to remember that it is in fact the Gray Catbird. When seen, its coloration is also easy to pick out – all gray with a distinct black cap and a rusty undertail covert area. They are quite inquisitive and come in readily to any squeaking sound. At such times they can be seen peering from the shrubs and bushes with their jet-black eye. Wherever there are dense shrubs and bushes this bird will be found, from mixed woodlands to brushy field edges and the backyard brush pile. In the fall a favorite spot is the large pokeweed stands that attract a multitude of birds. A walk through such a plot is sure to flush many catbirds or a least have them hop up to view the intruder before slipping back out of sight.

Catbirds belong to the family *Mimidae*, the mimics, which include the mockingbird, thrasher and the like. When its song is heard the harsh repetitive quality ties in with these relatives. It is not the mimic the others are, however, although within the jumble notes of a song some birds do interject some quite good mimicry.

The nest is placed deep in the tangles that make up the bird's home. A flattened saucer of sticks and grapevine bark strips with eggs of a beautiful greenish blue. Each year sees more and more catbirds remaining

FACTS AND FEATURES

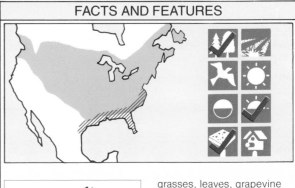

coyat eee ela toolee tee ta tee

Song A jumbed series of notes often harsh and with prolonged lispy endings.
Behavior Skulks in thickets.
Habitat Forest understorey, thickets, gardens, backyards.
Nest A bulky cup of sticks, grasses, leaves, grapevine shreds. The center of the cup is lined with rootlets, fibers and plant down.
Food About half animal matter — insects and their larvae, and half plant material — berries and seeds. At feeder takes orange halves, raisins and occasionally suet.

in the North for winter. At this time watch them sneak to the feeder for suet and raisins set out through severe period of weather. Seeds are taken only as an emergency food.

BROWN THRASHER *Toxostoma rufum*

The brown thrasher usually sings its distinctive song from a high perch, but it prefers to forage in the undergrowth of gardens, fields and hedges. It resembles a woodthrush but is larger and has a long tail, double white wing bars and a long curved bill. Length 11½ inches

AS THE FRESH WHORLS OF dogwood petals unfold and the elongate catkins of oaks come into full flower along the woodland edges and riverine forest trails, the Brown Thrasher's distinctive song can be heard over two thirds of the country. Though the notes have a harsh, raspy quality to them the diagnostic feature is that they are sung in couplets or triplets: *twee–twee toyou–toyou chack–chack wheep–wheep*.

Though a member of the mimic thrushes, it seldom imitates others as does its cousin the mockingbird, and when an attempt is made it is poor at best. To find the singer look for a perch high atop the tree and usually out in the open portion. It is a lovely bird, a rich foxy chestnut in color with heavy chestnut breast streaks. The tail is quite long and also of foxy hue. With head thrown back its whole body seems to reverberate as it sings.

But this is just a singing perch, not the nest area. To return to the nest site it will plunge from the tree tops down into the dense underbrush below. In the thickest of thickets it will place its flat cup-like nest of sticks interwoven with grape vine bark. The eggs are a light pale blue flecked with reddish spotting. In western areas the nest may even be placed on the ground and it is often subject to heavy predation. Thrashers will come to garden areas but are quite

FACTS AND FEATURES

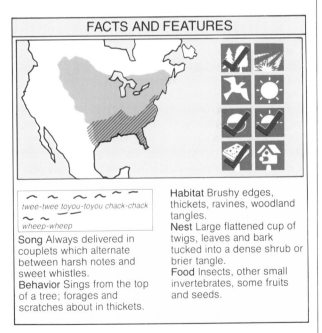

twee-twee toyou-toyou chack-chack
wheep-wheep

Song Always delivered in couplets which alternate between harsh notes and sweet whistles.
Behavior Sings from the top of a tree; forages and scratches about in thickets.

Habitat Brushy edges, thickets, ravines, woodland tangles.
Nest Large flattened cup of twigs, leaves and bark tucked into a dense shrub or brier tangle.
Food Insects, other small invertebrates, some fruits and seeds.

shy. In northern areas during the winter when an occasional bird will stay behind, suet is often a favorite item to help them survive until spring.

WRENTIT *Chamaea fasciata*

More often heard than seen, the wrentit lives in dense chaparral and sings in a loud, clear, descending trill. It has a short bill, a lightly streaked tan breast, a creamy eye and a long, unbarred and usually cocked tail. Length 6½ inches

THIS BIRD LIVES IN CHAPARRAL, a thick leaved, resilient Mediterranean-type scrub that clothes the hillsides and coastal bluffs of central and southern California. As the name implies it looks like a combination of a wren and a titmouse. It acts much like a titmouse as it works its way through the scrub in small groups and when seen its brown coloration and long cocked tail are reminiscent of a wren. In the southern portion of its range it is grayish, whereas in the northern area, it is a warm brown color.

The song is very distinctive, a loud staccato *pip–pip–pip* then a descending trailing off *ter–ter–ter–r–r–r*. The female also sings but just the initial *pip–pip–pip*.

Because of their secretive ways within the dense brush these birds are invariably heard before they are seen. Occasionally the northern form will appear in an area totally out of the norm, such as foraging high in an oak. If the bird is hard to see the nest is all but impossible to locate. Tucked into the base of a shrub deep in the thickets, it is a well-made cup of plant fibers; the eggs are as might be expected of a thrush – a lovely blue.

FACTS AND FEATURES

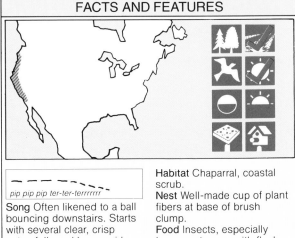

pip pip pip ter-ter-terrrrrr

Song Often likened to a ball bouncing downstairs. Starts with several clear, crisp notes followed by a rapid succession of down spiralling slurred notes.
Behavior Skulks; moves about in loose bands.

Habitat Chaparral, coastal scrub.
Nest Well-made cup of plant fibers at base of brush clump.
Food Insects, especially hymenopterans, with fleshy fruits making up over half the diet outside the breeding season.

Water Pipit *Anthus spinoletta*

FACTS AND FEATURES

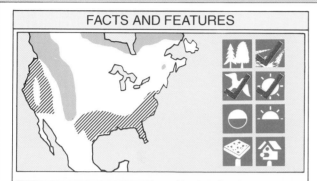

pip-pip-pipit cheedle zee

Song High pitched whistled notes followed by a thin, lisping series. When flushed delivers *pip-pip-it* call.
Behavior There is an aerial flight song but also sings from ground where it pumps tail up and down; flashes white in tail as it takes off; large fall and winter flocks.
Habitat Open country — tundra, mountains above the tree line, fields, coastal flats.
Nest Of grasses and sedges tucked into a grass hummock or rock crevice.
Food Insects and small invertebrates such as beach fleas.

TO MANY BIRDERS THE Water Pipit is a bird seen shuffling along a sandy beach, among the clods of a plowed field or flying overhead in a roller-coaster flight pattern calling its name *pip–pip–pipit*. To get to know this bird on its breeding grounds one must travel north or head up into the mountains, where it is a common nesting species. Within this tundra setting the flight song, made up of a series of high pitched *cheedle–zee* notes, is reminiscent of a jingle of keys. Lacking any singing posts of height the pipit has taken to the air for its place of territorial declaration. It circles high above often with a jerky flight pattern swinging in wide circles. Nearing the completion of the song period, which may last minutes, the bird plummets downward and lands on the tundra vegetation or rocky outcrop.

The Water Pipit walks about with tail pumping up and down and peers into every nook and cranny for food. This ranges from seeds to tiny invertebrates. In this situation its plumage is also seen to best advantage: a rich brown back with very faint streaking, and warm tawny buff underparts with a distinct necklace of brown streaking. The outer tail feathers are white. This is most easily seen as the bird flashes its tail open before landing.

The nesting range is quite unusual. In the West it is a bird of the High Rockies on up through Alaska. It nests throughout the tundra of Canada and then, oddly, a small nesting population exists on the flat tableland of Mount Katahdin in Maine, representing the only nestling site in the eastern United States.

In the fall and winter impressive flocks of thousands of birds can be seen in open fields across the southern portion of the United States and throughout Mexico and Central America.

The water pipit spends its summers in high mountain meadows and plains and moves to the water's edge in winter. It has a gray-brown back with faint streaking, light tan eye patches and underparts with darker streaks on its breast and flanks. It often bobs its tail when it walks. Length 7 inches

CEDAR WAXWING *Bombycilla cedrorum*

ON CRISP FALL MORNINGS one often hears the faint high-pitched trill of this species as great numbers pass overhead in loose flocks bound for the south. Breeding season has ended and now the wanderings begin. Nesting can take place anytime within a period from early summer to early fall depending on the range frequented. If one word was to sum up the Waxwing's lifestyle it would be "unpredictable." Simply to go afield and find a Waxwing is a most difficult task. More often than not they are found as they fly past or are stumbled upon feeding in a fruiting tree. Their food habits are also quite varied – the fruits of cedar, rowan, mulberry and pyracantha are favorites but a wide range of other shrubs and vines fruits are taken. In addition insects form a substantial part of their diet during the late summer. At this time the birds can be seen darting out over lakes, ponds and rivers grabbing up flying insects and returning to their perch. While "hawking" for insects and twisting and turning in flight they look more like a flycatcher than the trim beautifully colored bird perched atop a tree spire that one normally envisages.

With their sleek plumage, black mask, yellow-tipped tail and slim topknot crest they are unmistakable. The immature birds show heavy streaking on the underparts, less of a crest and only a dingy mask but the yellow tail tipping is diagnostic. The red, waxy tips can be seen when the birds are close. This modification of the secondary wing feather tips has a function as yet unknown other than to enhance the beauty of the bird.

The cedar waxwing varies its diet according to the season. During the winter, it eats berries, and it often nests late in the year when berries are available for the young. In the spring, it switches to insects. A warm brown bird with a crest and a black mask running through the eye, it is found throughout much of the country. Length 7 inches

FACTS AND FEATURES

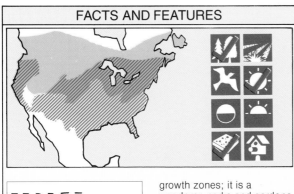

see-see-see-see

Song A high pitched trill on one plane.
Behavior Wanders about in groups; often seen chasing insects over ponds and rivers in the fall.
Habitat Open woodland, brushy areas, secondary growth zones; it is a wanderer, parks and gardens when on the move.
Nest Nest cup of grasses, rootlets, bark strips often covered with lichens in the north of its range. Nest placed in branched fork.
Food Mainly berries and seeds but will switch to insects when plentiful.

Although sedentary during the nesting season massive flocks can build in the fall and winter. It is at this time that berries on trees may be stripped in very short order, fermented berries leading to a drunken stupor. Many times I have seen these birds lined up on a fence or tree limb passing berries back and forth and swaying about or at times falling to the ground. They can be picked up and upon close inspection can be seen to be so inebriated as to not care that they are being held. After a short period of time the effect wears off and the birds continue to roam, their movements governed by availability of food.

The song is merely a high-pitched, soft, trilled whistle that once learned is not forgotten, and is often the giveaway that the birds are present in an area well before they are seen. On rare occasions the female has been recorded giving the weakened version of this penetrating song.

LOGGERHEAD SHRIKE *Lanius ludovicianus*

WALKING THE FENCE LINES of a local farm when I was a boy I came upon a rather macabre scene. The barbs of the wire held several specimens of dead animals. The most startling was a shrew hung by its shoulders as if tossed on a coat rack! Grasshoppers were in abundance. Perched atop a bush several yards away was the perpetrator of this mayhem, a Loggerhead Shrike, gray with a black mask, wings and tail. The strong, hooked bill used to snatch and snare the prey, the barbs of the wire or thorns of trees such as hawthorn are then used as the swords of final destruction. The food is left in place as a larder. Because of this unique feeding method not only is the nesting territory defended but winter territories are established to assure a food supply and storage.

The shrike's favored site is a perch atop a bush or snag where it can see over open fields and grasslands. When prey is sighted it drops from the perch, flies very low over the ground with a buzzy wingbeat and then swoops upward on to the next perch. In flight bold white wing patches can be seen in the primaries.

The song is a jumble of harsh squeaks and guttural warbles delivered from a perch near the nest site. The nest is a very bulky structure of twigs placed in a low bush or shrub.

The species has a wide range but has withdrawn from old areas of occupancy in the Northeast. The reason for this is as yet unclear. In the West and South Loggerhead Shrikes remain abundant and a typical part of the roadside aviafauna.

FACTS AND FEATURES

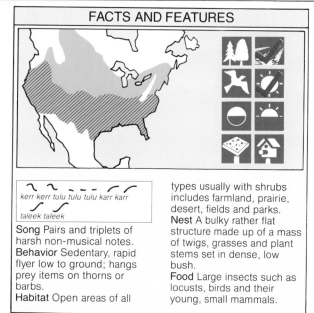

kerr kerr tulu tulu tulu karr karr

taleek taleek

Song Pairs and triplets of harsh non-musical notes.
Behavior Sedentary, rapid flyer low to ground; hangs prey items on thorns or barbs.
Habitat Open areas of all types usually with shrubs includes farmland, prairie, desert, fields and parks.
Nest A bulky rather flat structure made up of a mass of twigs, grasses and plant stems set in dense, low bush.
Food Large insects such as locusts, birds and their young, small mammals.

Perched high, the loggerhead swoops down to capture insects, small mammals or young birds and then impales them on thorny twigs ready for eating. In color, it resembles the mockingbird, but it has a short hooked beak, a black face mask and fast-beating wings. Length 9 inches

WARBLING VIREO *Vireo gilvus*

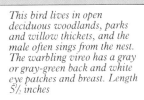

This bird lives in open deciduous woodlands, parks and willow thickets, and the male often sings from the nest. The warbling vireo has a gray or gray-green back and white eye patches and breast. Length 5½ inches

I WELL REMEMBER WAKING on January 1st in the mountains of Venezuela in great anticipation of the first bird of the New Year. As visions of racquet-tailed hummingbirds and the like soared through my mind the familiar call of the Warbling Vireo drifted in through the window. My visions of the most beautiful birds in the world vanished to be replaced by the reality of one of the drabbest! A uniform gray bird with no wing bars and a hint of an eyeline. At least the western form has a yellowish hue to its sides.

The Warbling Vireo frequents a wide variety of habitats, from the shade trees of a woodland lane to parks, gardens and cottonwoods along streams. It seems that if there are fairly large deciduous trees this bird will show up.

The song is a series of long warbling notes given in succession often on the same pitch. The male sings throughout the day from sunup to sunset and often sings on the nest! This is of course in direct opposition to the principles of nest camouflage and secrecy. As he takes up his turn he sings on and on. Certainly, this makes it one of the easiest of all birds' nests to find – track down the singing bird and you will see the nest!

The Warbling Vireo is very curious, and by making squeaking notes on the back of your hand can be enticed to come quite close, peering out of the leaves before giving a harsh, raspy *twee–twee* inquisitive scold. The species seems to show distinct peak and decline years, often with long intervening stretches.

FACTS AND FEATURES

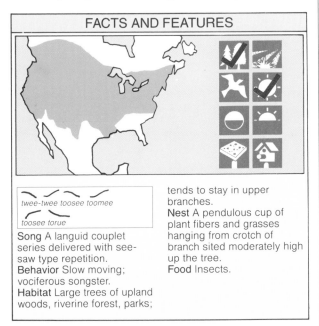

twee-twee toosee toomee

toosee torue

Song A languid couplet series delivered with see-saw type repetition.
Behavior Slow moving; vociferous songster.
Habitat Large trees of upland woods, riverine forest, parks; tends to stay in upper branches.
Nest A pendulous cup of plant fibers and grasses hanging from crotch of branch sited moderately high up the tree.
Food Insects.

Red-eyed Vireo *Vireo olivaceus*

FACTS AND FEATURES

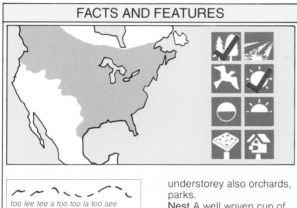

too lee tee a too too la too see

Song A series of two parted whistles that rock back and forth.
Behavior Deliberate yet slow moving; raises head feathers when disturbed.
Habitat Secondary growth woodlands with shrubby understorey also orchards, parks.
Nest A well woven cup of plant fibers and grasses covered with lichens and bound with spiderweb. Hangs from fork of outer shrub branches.
Food Mainly insects and small invertebrates.

ONE OF THE COMMONEST SONGBIRDS of the upland woods and one of the most constant singers – the Red-eyed Vireo is also listed as the world record holder for songs in one day with a reported 22,197 songs! Even on the warmest summer days when all seems still in the mixed eastern forests, the song of the Red-eyed Vireo labors on throughout the day. The song is a rhythm of short phrases *te–a–too tee–a–you* that seesaw back and forth with a rather raspy quality. As with all vireos, it moves about slowly in the canopy or sub-canopy vegetation with direct hops from limb to limb scanning the foliage for insects and their larvae.

A rather wide range in elevation may be chosen for the nest site. The nest is a well-made cup of grasses and fibers, covered with gray plant fibers and cobweb and hung from the crotch of a shrub or tree limb from 5-20ft off the ground. When a birder invades the bird's territory he will be greeted by the harsh scolds of the male, usually a raspy swishing mewing sound. The bird will be seen peering from the trees, leaning down with neck extended and head feathers slightly raised. The black line through the eye and the one edging the gray crown seem to focus the bird's intensity as it stares at the intruder. The red of the eye is also usually visible. Note there are no wingbars and the underparts are white. Young birds in the fall can be abundant migrants. The eye here is brownish and often the flanks are washed with yellow.

This species winters in the Central and South American tropics, where it needs the protection of the tropical forest habitat. With the loss of this forest we have already seen a decline in the total number of breeding birds. If forest destruction continues, what once was the most commonly seen songbird of the eastern forests may become a rarity within the next few decades.

This bird's song, a "question and answer" repetition, is a familiar sound from sunrise to sunset in upland woods throughout the eastern half of the country in summer. The red-eyed vireo prefers a steady diet of insects, but it will eat berries in the hardest of times. Length 6 inches

BELL'S VIREO *Vireo bellii*

BIRDING IN THE riverine willow thickets, bottomlands or mesquite areas found in the central and southwestern states, you are sure to encounter the unique song of Bell's Vireo. Listening carefully it sounds as if it is a question and answer series. The first part a distinct *cheedle cheedle chee?* with rising inflection followed by an emphatic drop in pitch *cheedle cheedle chew*. The song is given over and over as the bird moves about the thickets or lower areas of the trees. When finally glimpsed it is reminiscent of a ruby-crowned kinglet and is distinguished from the other vireo species by the less distinct wingbars and prominent eye-ring, which has a white line running to the bill from the eye.

This species comes in two basic color forms. The interior race, with distinctively yellowish underparts, and the race that reaches the West Coast which is markedly gray with a slight olive tint to the rump.

The suspended, cup-like nest is made of plant fibers, leaves and bark strips covered by plant down secured with spiderwebbing. It is placed in the fork of a branch and hangs down in the shape of an enlarged water droplet. This vireo suffers greatly from brood parasitism of brown-headed cowbirds, and the numbers appear to be on the decline in the western portion of its range.

Bell's vireo resembles the female ruby-brown kinglet, but it is larger and heavier and has a thicker bill. Those living in inland areas are brighter and yellower in color than their drab gray brothers living along the West Coast. Length 4¼ inches

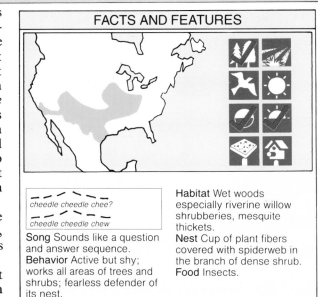

FACTS AND FEATURES

cheedle cheedle chee?
cheedle cheedle chew

Song Sounds like a question and answer sequence.
Behavior Active but shy; works all areas of trees and shrubs; fearless defender of its nest.

Habitat Wet woods especially riverine willow shrubberies, mesquite thickets.
Nest Cup of plant fibers covered with spiderweb in the branch of dense shrub.
Food Insects.

West Coast

Interior

KENTUCKY WARBLER *Oporornis formosus*

An inhabitant of damp, deciduous woodlands, the Kentucky warbler feeds and nests on the ground. It has a yellow eye ring and line above the eye, a black mustache, an olive-green back and bright yellow underparts. Some of its crown feathers are tipped with gray. Length 5¼ inches

WHILE WATCHING A PARADE of tropical species approaching a birdbath at the edge of a Costa Rican rainforest, a familiar sound came from the woodland edge. Into the bath popped a beautiful specimen of a male Kentucky Warbler. The note, a low *chuck* with a certain hollow quality, is a fairly common sound in the thickets of the South. Here in Costa Rica, it was in basically the same type of habitat as its northern breeding grounds, where it also spends a large amount of time foraging on the ground. It overturns leaves and searches the base of shrubs for small insects, egg cases and larval forms.

In the spring, the Kentucky Warbler returns to the North where its loud ringing song is heard once again. The song, although interpreted many ways, is basically a repeated, rolling *tory – tory – tory – tory* or *turtle, turtle, turtle, turtle*. The bird sings from a low perch and though apparently right in front of you, can be difficult to locate. Famed ornithologist Roger Tory Peterson states, "Learn the song – 10 Kentuckies are heard for every one seen." When it is seen it is easy to identify with its bright yellow underparts, olive greenish back and black sideburns running down from the eye.

The nest is a bulky cup of leaves and grasses found on the ground, and often tucked under an overhang. On occasion it will be placed a foot or so off the ground in the base of a shrub. This bird is a true skulker of the thicket and it is a challenge to get a good view of it. Once you have seen this handsome warbler, however, the hunt will have seemed well worth it.

FACTS AND FEATURES

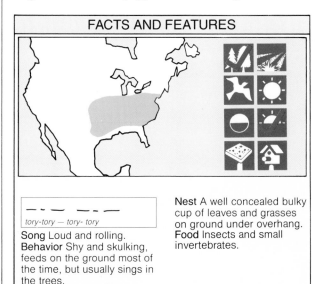

tory-tory — tory- tory

Song Loud and rolling.
Behavior Shy and skulking, feeds on the ground most of the time, but usually sings in the trees.
Habitat Boggy woodlands, bushy swamps.

Nest A well concealed bulky cup of leaves and grasses on ground under overhang.
Food Insects and small invertebrates.

103

Northern Parula Warbler *Parula americana*

FACTS AND FEATURES

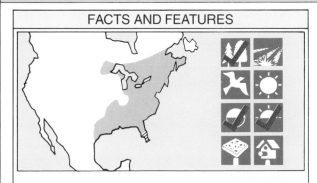

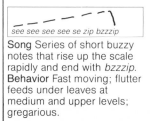

see see see see se zip bzzzip

Song Series of short buzzy notes that rise up the scale rapidly and end with *bzzzip.*
Behavior Fast moving; flutter feeds under leaves at medium and upper levels; gregarious.

Habitat Coniferous forest with *Usnea* lichen and mixed woods with Spanish moss; on migration all forest types.
Nest Cup of fibers in *Usnea* or Spanish moss cup.
Food Adult insects, their eggs and larvae.

THIS DIMINUTIVE WARBLER is familiar to every watcher in the East who heads out to see the return of the warbler flocks each spring. It is a common species in migration and its diagnostic call makes it easy to locate. The call is a series of buzzy notes that climb the scale and then finish with an abrupt *zip*. The bird itself is usually found fairly high off the ground and usually out near the outermost branches, where it hangs acrobatically like a chickadee foraging for food. It will also study leaves from below then flutter up to pick off a small caterpillar.

It is a striking-looking warbler: a blue-gray back saddle with olive, bright white wing bars and a broken eye ring. The throat and breast are a bright yellow, crossed by a band of rusty orange and blue. It is very active, and this, coupled with its small size, allows it to disappear quickly behind new leaves, making it extremely difficult to see.

It is found as a summer resident over a wide range extending from the maritime provinces of Canada south to Florida and the Texas coast. This scale of range can result in what appears to be a skewed distribution because nesting is often spotty. In the North it prefers the coniferous forests where the amazing little cup nest is made of the lichen *Usnea* tucked within a dense *Usnea* clump. In the South the draping masses of Spanish moss are to their liking, and the near-invisible nest is placed within the gray masses. Where neither of these growths are found the nesting choice varies, but usually an evergreen habitat is chosen.

Small in size with a gray-blue back, yellow throat, narrow eye ring and two white wing bars, the northern parula differs in appearance from all other warblers. The male also has dark bands across its chest and a faint yellow patch on its back. These birds are numerous in mature deciduous and coniferous woodlands. Length 4½ inches

Yellow Warbler *Dendroica petechia*

THROUGHOUT MOST OF NORTH AMERICA where there is wet habitat in the form of a flood plain, willow bottomland, or moist tundra hillside, the loud and clear *sweet–sweet–sweet–oh–so–sweet* song of the Yellow Warbler is sure to be heard. In the spring when singing is at its peak these birds can be seen in hot pursuit of aggressors crossing territorial lines or, with head thrown back in song, perched on the uppermost branches of a shrub. Yellow forms can be seen darting here and there as the fever of nesting activity increases. During these periods the males sing while collecting materials such as the fluff of willow seeds and bark fibers woven together to form the outside of the nest. The sturdy little cup that is placed in a crotch or suspended slightly is lined with grasses and is resilient enough to be seen through the winter following a nesting season; at this time it is interesting to explore such a nest especially if it appears to be exceptionally elongated.

The nests of the Yellow Warblers are favorite sites for the parasitic brown-headed cowbird to lay its eggs. However, unlike many other species, the Yellow Warbler on occasion will notice the undesirable egg and simply build a "floor" over it, increasing the nest's height and re-lay.

Viewed closely the birds show more than just the brilliant yellow. For example, the male's yellow on the upper breast at times approaches an orange color and lining the whole chest and underbelly are rich chestnut-red lines. The eye is a jet bead of black. This also applies to the female with her olive back and less brilliant yellow underparts. Note also that these birds often spread their tails, exposing white corner markings.

FACTS AND FEATURES

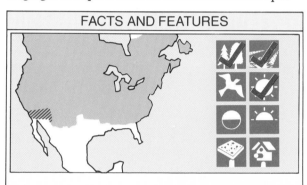

sweet sweet sweet Oh so sweet

Song Very rapid and pure in quality.
Behavior Very active in defending its territory; sings constantly especially in the morning.
Habitat Wet areas, especially with willows; open woodland, parkland.
Nest A fine built cup of plant fibers, grasses and down covered with willow threads and spiderwebs. Placed in crotch of a small tree.
Food Mainly insects, some spiders and other small invertebrates.

The male is a brilliant yellow bird with a rust-colored beak and rust belly streaks and black button eyes; the female is drabber and lacks the belly streaks. The yellow warbler falls frequent victim to the parasitic brown-headed cowbird. Length 5 inches

CHESTNUT-SIDED WARBLER *Dendroica pensylvanica*

Numerous in open deciduous thickets or shrubs, this bird's bold chestnut brown sides make it easy to distinguish from all other birds except the bay-breasted warbler. Its identity can be confirmed by its yellow crown, black line through the eye, black mustache, heavily streaked back and two yellow wing bars. Length 5 inches

WHILE WALKING THE FIELD EDGE or second growth area in the early spring one will very often be greeted by a song that is best interpreted as a welcome: *please, please please to meet cha*. The greeter is the Chestnut-sided Warbler, a bird of the lower branches and tangle. It is a most striking bird in breeding plumage with a striking lemon-yellow cap, and a black line through the eye and cheek area running into the rich chestnut brown of the sides. The underparts are pure white, the back streaked with light yellow. During the fall migration it becomes a drab member of the migrating feeding flock; white below with greenish back and pure white underparts. There is often a smudge color to the sides. The eye is large and the cap has a very greenish color. As on the breeding grounds it tends to forage low and frequent brushy thickets and slash areas.

It is interesting to note in Audubon's writings that apparently he only encountered the Chestnut-sided but once in all of his great travels. Since Audubon's time and with the trailing off of farming, more fields are left to go fallow and this has had a great impact on increasing this species' numbers. Powerlines have aided the bird by its continual management of the scrubby areas below the lines.

The nest is a beautiful cup of grasses, rootlets and plant fibers placed very low to the ground in a shrub or low bush. Even the eggs are diagnostic as they have distinct ring or markings around the larger end.

The late-season song is a much more muted call, a soft *tsip* or louder *chip*. With the coming of the fall the population wings its way south to Central and South America where it occupies a place quite unlike that at "home," for here it tends to spend a lot of time quite high in the trees, often in the sub-canopy. Within its winter range the low-level niche is occupied by resident species, hence the switch to a new zone of activity.

FACTS AND FEATURES

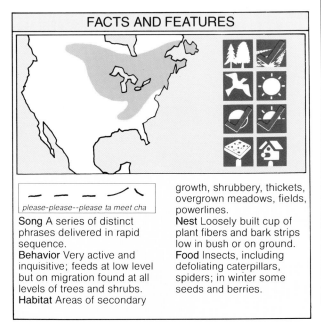

please-please--please ta meet cha

Song A series of distinct phrases delivered in rapid sequence.
Behavior Very active and inquisitive; feeds at low level but on migration found at all levels of trees and shrubs.
Habitat Areas of secondary growth, shrubbery, thickets, overgrown meadows, fields, powerlines.
Nest Loosely built cup of plant fibers and bark strips low in bush or on ground.
Food Insects, including defoliating caterpillars, spiders; in winter some seeds and berries.

BLACK-THROATED BLUE WARBLER *Dendroica caerulescens*

THE MASTERING OF BIRD SONG is a long slow process. There appear to be no ready shortcuts. One must simply hear a song over and over to master it – yet so many sound so similar. Therefore, it is most rewarding for the beginning birder to master a warbler song in very short order. Such is the song of the beautiful Black-throated Blue. It is very distinct in its uttering of *I am so la – zeee*! This trails on up the scale and ends with distinctive punctuation. To find the songster look at fairly low understory or the lowest branches of trees in mixed woodlands, wet areas and wooded cool ravines.

The male is spectacular with its deep blue cap and back in sharp contrast to black face, throat and sides and its pure white underbelly. Make note of the perfect square of white in the wing. This mark in itself is enough to identify this species in all plumages and for both sexes. For example the female is a dull brownish with buff-tinted underparts and the white primary spot stands out. Be on the alert because it can take a fair amount of watching to see this spot. But don't feel frustrated in waiting for your information, both Wilson and Audubon felt the female was a different species from the male and even labeled her so, calling her the Pine Swamp Warbler.

The nest is quite large for such a small bird. A fork in an evergreen shrub is most often chosen with the nest usually being placed within 3ft of the ground. It is made of leaves, bark shreds, twigs, mosses and even small wood fragments. Only the spiderweb covering holds things in place.

FACTS AND FEATURES

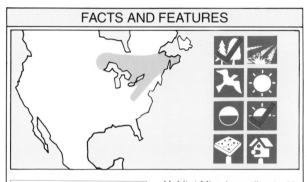

I'm so lazy

Song Of a buzzy, wheezy quality, distinct at first then rapidly rising up the scale.
Behavior Forages at all levels but most common in the understory; often perches with wings partly open.

Habitat Mixed woodland with understory.
Nest Bulky cup of leaves, sticks and bark shreds.
Food Small insects, grubs and larvae and spiders.

The blue back, black cheeks, throat and sides with white underparts and small white wing patches make the male of this species unmistakable. Length 5¼ inches

Pine Warbler *Dendroica pinus*

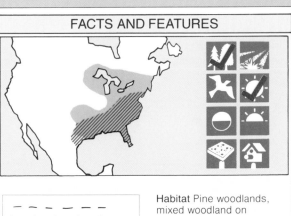

FACTS AND FEATURES

chee chee chee chee chee

Song A continuous musical trill of chip notes.
Behavior Active high in the canopy; early arrival on spring feeding grounds.

Habitat Pine woodlands, mixed woodland on migration.
Nest A cup of twigs, bark strips and pine needles high in evergreen on a limb.
Food Insects, pine seeds and some berries.

During migration, this bird can be seen in orchards and mixed woodlands, but it settles in pine woods to breed. It can be distinguished by its yellow breast, large white wing bars, white belly and undertail and white spots on its outer tail feathers. Length 5½ inches

ON SCORCHING SUMMER DAYS in the dry, sandy pine barrens of the East all is still under the blazing sun, all except for one bird whose solitary song dominates the atmosphere. The dry, staccato trill of the Pine Warbler is repeated over and over throughout the day no matter how hot it gets. Between bouts of singing the bird can be seen working the upper pine branches in search of insects, stopping now and then to throw its head back and pour forth the rattling song. It is one of the least distinctive of our warblers, though the male has a rich yellow breast with faint side and flank streaks in spring. One field mark difficult to see is the unmarked back that helps separate it from look-alike species, especially in the fall. It has often been stated that if you are looking at a museum collection of relatively unmarked warblers and your feeling is what a drab lot they are, then more than likely it is a collection of Pine Warblers.

It is a permanent resident in the pine flatlands of the South, and one of the earliest migrants in the northeast, its buzzy trill heard by the first week of April. As the name implies it is a pinewood species, but more specifically it prefers burnt areas with sparse growths of pitch pine and scrub oak. So, in order to be a prime habitat for this bird, pinewoods need to have a major fire every 10 years or so. In some areas, the problem has been solved by a policy of controlled burning to rejuvenate the woods, which has benefited the Pine Warbler greatly. But in other areas, fire prevention has drastically altered the landscape and ousted the Pine Warbler from its favored habitat. Fortunately, it is still a relatively common and resilient species.

BLACKPOLL WARBLER *Dendroica striata*

FACTS AND FEATURES

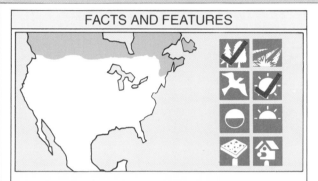

tsee — see-see-see see-see

Song High pitched and penetrating.
Behavior Stays fairly high in the trees, works its way out along limbs.
Habitat Coniferous forest during breeding season, mixed forest during migration.
Nest Cup of twigs, rootlets and lichens placed fairly high in the limb of a conifer on flat portion of limb.
Food Various small, winged insects, larval forms and egg cases, spiders.

THIS WARBLER is a true embodiment of the northern coniferous forests common throughout Canada and Alaska where its penetrating high lisping *tsee — see — see —* *see — see* call is sung throughout the day. Within the lower 48 states it nests only in the extreme northern section of New England, and northern New York.

It usually delivers its song from atop an evergreen, and its whole body seems to vibrate as it sits, head thrown back, delivering these penetrating notes. The spring birds are easy to identify with their bold black and white pattern and all-black cap or poll; the cheeks are white. Fall birds, however, can frustrate the warbler watcher faced with a complex of seemingly look-alike olive species. But note the wingbars, yellow tint to throat, white undertail and orange feet! Most of the migrants pass east of the Mississippi River in both the spring and fall movement, even those birds going to Alaska. The southern movement can be spectacular as birds prepare early in August to depart the East Coast for a direct, non-stop flight to South America. In preparation for their long haul they fatten up first to double their normal body weight. Out into the night, far off the coast, they pick up tail winds (as far out as Bermuda) that will assist them on this final leg of their journey on to South America. This is a most remarkable feat. Although they spend more than half their year in the tropics, we still think of them as birds of the northern forests.

Numerous in coniferous forests, the blackpoll warbler differs from the black and white warbler and the black-throated gray warbler in its black cap and white throat and cheeks. Its underparts are white, heavily streaked with black and the undertail is white. It also has two prominent white wing bars. Length 5½ inches

BLACK-AND-WHITE WARBLER *Mniotilta varia*

♂

♀

The only warbler with black and white plumage and a white stripe through its crown, this bird prefers deciduous woodlands. It searches the trunks and branches of trees for insect eggs and larvae and can often be seen hanging upside down beneath a branch. It is one of the first birds to arrive at the northern part of its range in the spring. Length 5¼ inches

WARBLER WATCHING seems not only to attract a large portion of people but also to terrorize them. The cry in the spring is always "I hope they get here before the leaves come out so I can see them!" and in the fall, "What is that darn greenish colored warbler?" Therefore, a species such as the Black-and-White is a welcome respite to both problems. In the spring it is easily seen, as it is a bark gleaner, and spends all of its time working on the trunk or limbs of the trees, often in clear view. In addition its work takes it down to low levels in the understory trees for virtually eye-to-eye views. The Black-and-White remains in its "zebra" plumage throughout the year, though it is less intense in the fall, and is therefore a warbler that even the most novice birders can identify with confidence.

It is the nuthatch of the warbler group and this allows it to obtain food in a place that lacks competition from other warblers. In fact it often moves with groups of warblers and chickadees during these foraging forays.

The song is fairly easy to remember. A drawn out series of two part, wheezy notes *wee-see wee-see wee-see*. I often liken it to the sound of a small car starting. Occasionally it will break into a more complicated song, especially on territory. The nest is placed directly on the ground, usually in a concavity next to a rock or tree base. The preference of habitat is deciduous or mixed forest with damp woodlands.

FACTS AND FEATURES

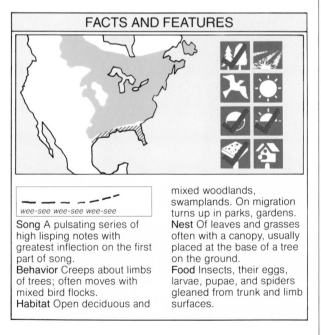

wee-see wee-see wee-see

Song A pulsating series of high lisping notes with greatest inflection on the first part of song.
Behavior Creeps about limbs of trees; often moves with mixed bird flocks.
Habitat Open deciduous and mixed woodlands, swamplands. On migration turns up in parks, gardens.
Nest Of leaves and grasses often with a canopy, usually placed at the base of a tree on the ground.
Food Insects, their eggs, larvae, pupae, and spiders gleaned from trunk and limb surfaces.

WILSON'S WARBLER *Wilsonia pusilla*

PERPETUAL MOTION is one way to describe a Wilson's Warbler. During migration they dart here and there seeking small insects, hopping from limb to limb, never seeming to sit still long enough for the birder to get a good look. This is complicated by the fact that they tend to stay low to the ground and frequent dense thickets. When they do pop into view they certainly are one of the easiest warblers to identify – bright yellow with an olive back and a jet black cap. They like to flutter feed, darting up beneath a leaf with wings beating to snap up an insect, and then dropping back.

Their song is an unstructured series of slurred notes dropping rapidly in pitch, almost as if they wanted to hurry up and finish the song, so as to get back to eating. To the easterner, this is a bird of migration, whereas in the West the significant nesting population makes this species much more common. The nesting range extends up into Alaska where Wilson's Warbler is abundant, nesting in the endless alder thickets that are so much a feature of that spectacular land. Although the bird may be easy to see, the nest is difficult to locate. A cup of mosses, grasses and rootlets, it is usually tucked into a hillside crevice, or at the base of a shrub such as dwarf willows. Only the female incubates, and the male is continuously visible on the territory. It is

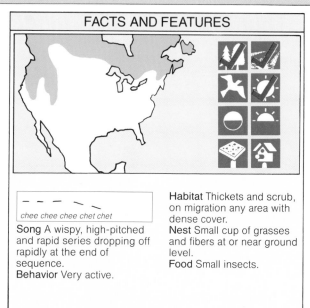

FACTS AND FEATURES

chee chee chee chet chet

Song A wispy, high-pitched and rapid series dropping off rapidly at the end of sequence.
Behavior Very active.

Habitat Thickets and scrub, on migration any area with dense cover.
Nest Small cup of grasses and fibers at or near ground level.
Food Small insects.

difficult to follow him to the nest site during his infrequent visits to the female, and finding the nest is a real challenge.

A frequently sighted bird of the West, Wilson's warbler lives in willow thickets, bogs, damp woodlands and along the edges of streams. It has a dark eye on an otherwise plain face, an olive-green back and yellow underparts. The female lacks tail spots. Length 4¾ inches

AMERICAN REDSTART *Setophaga ruticilla*

AUDUBON PROCLAIMED THEM "the butterflies of the bird-world," and certainly they draw as much attention as another group of birds, the warblers. The Redstart is often very butterfly-like, flitting around among the foliage and dancing along the limb, switching its body back and forth with each hop. Tail fanning in and out or flutter feeding under a leaf, it pursues its prey to the ground in an erratic flight, very like a leaf tumbling to the ground. Bedecked in black and orange, the male Redstart is a most handsome warbler. It is one of the earliest warblers to arrive, and one of the best known because it is so common, and distinct yellow or orange squares in its tail makes it easy to identify in all plumages.

During spring migration the hurried, buzzy song is a common forest and woodland edge sound. The territory for nesting is usually a heavily thicketed area with water nearby, be it swamp or stream. The nest is a beautifully woven structure; a solid cup, placed securely in the crotch of a shrub or sapling and most often quite close to the ground. Made of plant fibers and coated with cobwebs, any decoration is of plant fibers, lichens and animal hair. The Redstart's nest seems to be a favorite of the parasitic brown-headed cowbird, and on several occasions I have seen this diminutive warbler stuffing larvae after larvae into the gaping mouth of its massive foster youngster.

In the fall they change into their protective colors – basically gray plumage, orange shoulders and flanks – and often seem like the most abundant warbler on migration. Searching through a large migrant flock, the birder often is frustrated to find eight of the 10 flitting warblers checked in search for the big "rarity" to be this species.

A "flutter" feeder, the American redstart hovers beneath a leaf or captures insects in midair. It also hops along branches swinging its body from side to side. Mature males are jet black with orange markings that show brilliantly when they fan their tails. Length 5 inches

♀

♂

FACTS AND FEATURES

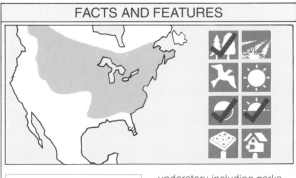

zee zeee zee zee soowe

Song A hurried buzzy song, a complex of lisping notes.
Behavior Very active, flutter feeds or works its way along a limb, tail fanned, swinging from side to side.
Habitat Deciduous woodland with scrub and thicket understory including parks and gardens with shrubs and young tree growth.
Nest A well woven elongated cup of plant fibers and rootlets bound by spiderweb in crotch of scrub.
Food Insects, often small flying forms and spiders. Some fruit and seeds.

PROTHONOTARY WARBLER *Protonotaria citrea*

A PROTHONOTARY is a keeper of records in the College of Prothonotaries Apostolic of the Roman Catholic Church. Their robe color is a brilliant orange yellow, and one that the brilliant plumage of this warbler was compared with when first identified. Their range extends from Florida north as far as the Great Lakes but in many people's minds this bird means Spanish moss-draped stumps of southern Bayou country and the low, flooded swamplands of the South. For the New Englander this warbler is always a rare treat in the spring; and on Point Pelee in Ontario the crowd eagerly await their first sighting in the peak of spring migration. It is quite a wanderer and has appeared virtually coast to coast at one time or another during migration periods.

It has the uncharacteristic warbler habit of nesting in a natural tree cavity or old abandoned woodpecker working. No other eastern warbler does this. The site chosen is fairly close to the ground usually next to a backwater pool or sluggish stream. In this setting the loud and repetitive *sweet–weet–weet–weet* is staccato and on an even pitch. As with many other warblers, during the peak of the breeding season this bird will burst into the air and flutter about singing a canary-like song while hovering with feet dangling, usually near the nest site.

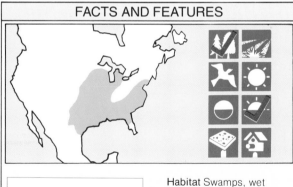

This bird has a golden yellow head and underparts, white undertail, blue-gray wings and a blue-gray tail with large white patches. It lives in damp woods and along the edges of streams. Length 5½ inches

FACTS AND FEATURES

sweet-weet-weet-weet-weet

Song A sweet series of notes maintained at the same pitch.
Behavior Stays low and near water.

Habitat Swamps, wet lowlands, bayous.
Nest In natural cavity or old woodpecker hole.
Food Small insects.

OVENBIRD *Seiurus aurocapillus*

ONE OF THE MOST FAMILIAR woodland sounds for two-thirds of the United States is the loud sharp *teacher–teacher–teacher–teacher* rising up the scale as it intensifies. For some it heralds the return of the wood warblers to the summer forest. For others it represents a woodland voice along with the red-eyed vireo to punctuate the still, humid air of the hot summer wood. It certainly is one of the warbler songs that is most quickly learned by the beginning bird enthusiast. Depending on the bird the calls may vary from an emphasis on the first note or the last. But in all cases the distinct *teacher* sound is hard to mistake.

The bird itself is more thrush-like than warbler-like with an olive brown back and spotted underparts when first seen walking about on the forest floor. A closer view reveals the orange head stripe bordered by black, clearly seen when the bird is excited as it erects these central head feathers. Though they do sing while walking about, they seem to prefer to find a branch, not too high above the leaf-strewn floor, to arch their head back and pour forth their penetrating song.

The name "ovenbird" comes from the nest, very well hidden among the leaves on the ground. I dare say that if one went in search of an ovenbird nest it would be a long, hard and often fruitless endeavor. More often than not the nest is located accidentally as you walk in the woods and are startled by a small bird fluttering up at your feet. At times they will tumble through the forest duff as if injured in an attempt to lead you away from the nest. A little time spent should reveal the domed-over, side-entry nest very reminiscent of a Dutch oven and hence the source of the bird's name. It is well-made of leaves and grasses

and lined with hair. The entry to the nest is a mere slit, making the whole structure seem like a bump in the leaves. The adult lands near the nest and walks a short way to the side entrance before slipping from sight.

Though the nest may be difficult for the birder to locate, the parasitic cowbird seems to find this species much to its liking and the Ovenbird's nest falls victim to a cowbird's egg more commonly than most other forest species. In addition, being a ground nest, many eggs and young are lost to ground predators.

FACTS AND FEATURES

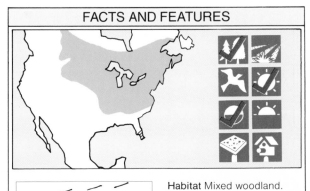

teacher-teacher-teacher-teacher

Song A loud series of distinct phrases rising in intensity. Also a more gushing evening song.
Behavior Forages about forest floor; will call from understory; tree.

Habitat Mixed woodland.
Nest Domed nest of grasses with side entrance.
Food Insects and other invertebrates.

Usually seen walking along the ground in deciduous woodlands, the ovenbird has a dull orange crown bordered by black stripes, white underparts streaked with black, and pink legs. It resembles the waterthrush but has a clear white eye ring rather than an eye stripe. Length 6 inches

LOUISIANA WATERTHRUSH *Seiurus motacilla*

IN THE EARLY SPRING when new leaves of beech add a fresh green glow to ravine hillsides and the streams are filled with the spring rains, the rich, full song of the Louisiana Waterthrush is a most welcome sound, indicating that spring has indeed returned. It is one of the earliest of the warblers returning from its Central American and Mexican haunts where it has overwintered. The song is introduced by three clear whistles and is followed by a series of sweet jumbled notes that cascade down the scale. The bird that produces such a distinctive and loud song is not always that easily seen.

The ringing quality of the song often makes it hard to pinpoint the singer, who may deliver the song from a low tree limb, high in the upper branches of a ravine side tree or from the rocks along the water's edge.

When finally seen it is easy to understand why this species of warbler was named a Waterthrush. It does look very thrush-like – but sleek – and teeters its tail up and down as it walks. The back color is brown and the underparts are heavily streaked. Over the eye is a distinct white line and the pure white throat separates this species from its look–alike cousin, the northern waterthrush. If one spends some time in the bird's haunts it is not difficult to find them foraging for food, diligently walking by a stream edge flicking over leaves and walking out into the water to turn over exposed debris for insects and other small invertebrates. And all the while, the tail and hind portion keep bobbing up and down. If you are very fortunate you may see the bird make its way to the nest, most difficult to locate. Tucked into an overhang of bank, or placed among the tangled roots of an upturned stump by the water's edge, the nest is a cup of leaves, grasses and rootlets that blends incredibly well with the selected nest sites. Usually one sees the bird working along and then it seems to vanish into the background. Close inspection will reveal that it has settled on the nest and is peering out at you.

Just as it is an early arrival in spring for a warbler, it departs remarkably early in late summer. By late August most Louisiana Waterthrushes are well on their way back to their Latin American haunts to winter before bringing the "word" back to the birders that spring is on its way.

FACTS AND FEATURES

see-see-see-too la see de

Song Two parted, introduced by three clear whistled notes followed by a rapid series of clear bubbling notes rolling down the scale. Sometimes sings in flight.
Behavior Bobs tail as it walks about; feeds at stream edge.

Habitat Breeds near flowing streams; other wet areas on migration.
Nest Bulky cup of grasses, leaves and rootlets tucked into bank or upturned stump.
Food Invertebrates such as worms, as well as insects and their larvae.

This bird lives near streams in wooded ravines or in woodland swamps. It bobs its tail as it walks. Similar in appearance to the northern waterthrush, it can be distinguished by its white eye stripe, plain white throat and larger bill. Its legs are flesh-colored. Length 6 inches

CONNECTICUT WARBLER *Oporornis agilis*

Best distinguished from MacGillivray's warbler and the mourning warbler by its bold white eye ring. The male has a gray hood while the female's is brown. A relatively rare bird, the Connecticut warbler lives in damp woodlands and spruce bogs. Length 5¼ inches

BEING A RESIDENT OF CONNECTICUT, one question asked by those unfamiliar with the bird's range is: "Of course you have nesting Connecticut Warblers near you?" The answer, of course, is no! It was named by Wilson who first saw it in Connecticut and to this day it remains a scarce migrant during the fall. As it passes through, skulking in the pepperbush and touch-me-not thickets of the wetlands, it often goes unnoticed. In the spring it is a migrant west of the Appalachian Mountains and is practically unknown on the eastern seaboard during this period. While it spends the spring and summer in the US it resides almost entirely in Canada. Outside of the western Great Lake states it breeds nowhere else in the United States.

The Connecticut Warbler's favorite haunts are spruce bogs and wet woodlands. Its presence on territory is announced by a loud clear ringing song that starts *blit blit* moving on to a rapid *see-to-it see-to-it*.

It is a bird of the bog floor and walks about, much like an ovenbird, in search of small insects and spiders. The distinct gray hood that crosses the chest coupled with the complete eye-ring identifies this large warbler. Also note how long the undertail coverts are, extending to nearly the end of the tail. If seen walking about, also note the jerking of the head and the cocking of the tail.

To really get to know this bird expect to spend long hours afield in wet habitat. Insight into such a species, known but to a few, can be a most self-rewarding endeavor.

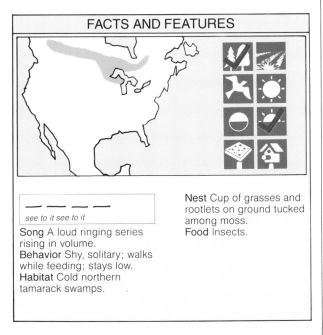

FACTS AND FEATURES

see to it see to it

Song A loud ringing series rising in volume.
Behavior Shy, solitary; walks while feeding; stays low.
Habitat Cold northern tamarack swamps.

Nest Cup of grasses and rootlets on ground tucked among moss.
Food Insects.

116

COMMON YELLOWTHROAT *Geothlypis trichas*

FACTS AND FEATURES

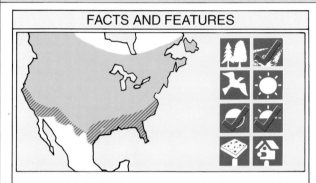

twitchity twitchity twitchity

Song Series of rapid explosive calls with an emphasis on the first part *twitch---ity*.
Behavior Very active but skulks amongst vegetation; cocks tail.

Habitat Damp fields, dense thickets, cattail marshes, mangroves in South.
Nest Rather large and often cone shaped of grasses, large leaves, bark strips, on or near the ground.
Food Insects.

THE LOUD PLEASANT SONG *twitchity, twitchity, twitchity* of the Common Yellowthroat is a familiar sound of wetlands and coastal marshes throughout the United States and southern Canada. In action the bird is reminiscent more of a wren than a warbler. As it works its way about in the dense underbrush grasping the twigs from the side and peering out through protected openings, it even holds its tail cocked at an upward angle. During these times it usually scolds constantly with a sharp *chick–chick*. The male is unmistakable with black mask, yellow throat and olive upper parts. The female lacks the mask but has an all-yellow throat, marking the separation between it and look-alikes such as the mourning warbler. There are several races but all have the same basic color pattern.

During the mating season the male often bursts into the air with a fluttering flight, cocks its body upward and soars about giving a rather jumbled song of mismatched notes before plunging back into the thickets. This "ecstasy song" is performed by other warblers and seems to be a reinforcement of territorial behavior.

One of the easiest birds to identify, the male has a black face mask and yellow throat. The female also has a yellow throat, but her face is olive green. An insect eater, the common yellowthroat lives in marshes and thickets throughout the country in summer and in the South year-round. Length 5 inches

YELLOW-BREASTED CHAT *Icteria virens*

ALTHOUGH FOUND FROM COAST TO COAST many people are not at all familiar with this, our largest warbler. This is largely because it is a very shy species, and tends to be solitary outside the breeding season.

In many respects the Yellow-breasted Chat is quite unique. At 7½ in, it looks more like a type of thrush than a warbler. Although its brilliant underbelly would seem to make it a species that could be picked out easily, it inhabits the densest tangles from grape vines ensnarled in brushy thickets to a labyrinth of impenetrable greenbrier. And even when approached they often view the intruder over the shoulder so not to expose the brightness of the breast. As if these were not enough quirks, they love to sing all night – a series of loud harsh *chack chack–ree–chip chip–twee twee*, on and on in an endless flow of harsh jumbled notes. They also call during the day using a variety of harsh notes, clucks, gurgles and whistles. This is either from a perch, or wings dangling they launch themselves into the air and with buoyant wingbeats and legs hanging cast out an elaborate jumble of song.

The nest is usually placed in the middle of a brush thicket. It is a rather bulky stick structure loosely put together and flattening very quickly once the adult visits continually with food.

In northern areas some birds will stay back during

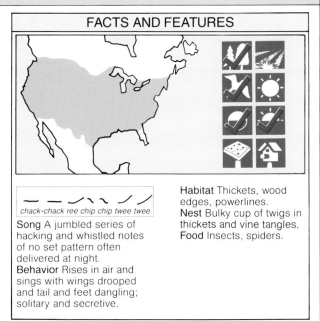

FACTS AND FEATURES

chack-chack ree chip chip twee twee

Song A jumbled series of hacking and whistled notes of no set pattern often delivered at night.
Behavior Rises in air and sings with wings drooped and tail and feet dangling; solitary and secretive.

Habitat Thickets, wood edges, powerlines.
Nest Bulky cup of twigs in thickets and vine tangles.
Food Insects, spiders.

the winter. It is then they may sneak to a backyard feeder to steal a morsel of suet for high energy. This is an interesting species and it is too bad people do not get a chance to see it more easily.

A large bird with a long tail and a thick bill, the yellow breasted chat has a gray-green back, wings and tail, bright yellow underparts except for a white belly and undertail. It likes to hide in deciduous thickets and underbrush. Length 7½ inches

PYRRHULOXIA *Cardinalis sinuatus*

THIS BIRD'S MOST UNUSUAL NAME, if broken down into its Greek and Latin parts means "fiery-red bird with a crooked bill." What a striking bird it is, with brilliant red on its face, throat and belly and a large, yellow, strongly curved parrot-like bill. Birders traveling to the Southwest for the first time often think that they are looking at a cardinal on seeing the female.

However, the grayness of the body, the yellow bill and the exceptionally long crest with its bright red tip quickly eliminates the confusion.

This species has a limited range in the Southwest, but where found it is a permanent resident and is usually quite common. It covers a wide range of habitats from woodland edges to dry desert areas, mesquite shrub to garden thicket. In lifestyle and activities, the Pyrrhuloxia is very similar to a cardinal, as it hops about feeding on a wide variety of seeds.

The nest, a fairly well-made cup of twigs, rootlets and plant fibers is tucked into a dense thicket usually not too far above ground. At the approach of an intruder these birds become very alarmed and loudly scold man or animal with harsh *chink* notes, their crest raised to a near-vertical position. After breeding they tend to form into small bands and move into agricultural areas to search out concentrated sources of seed. During such periods they will adopt suburban settings, and come in to the garden to feed. Like its cousin the cardinal, sunflower seeds provide a main attraction.

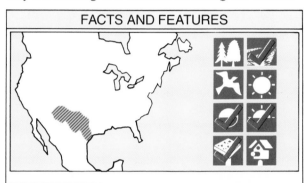

FACTS AND FEATURES

see-too see too — pew you pew you

Song Very similar to the clear ringing notes of a cardinal. Female has a weaker song.
Behavior Stalks in thickets; but will pop into view to see intruder; will forage out on open grass areas. Raises crest straight up when alarmed.
Habitat Weedy thickets, grassland edges, gardens.
Nest Compact cup of twigs, grasses and plant fibers in a dense shrub.
Food A wide variety of seeds; will visit feeder for oil, sunflower seed and cracked corn.

Like the cardinal, the pyrrhuloxia has a red crest and red on its face, throat, underparts and tail. But it also has a gray back and a thick, curved, pale yellow bill. The female has a gray tail and more gray on its body than the male. It prefers to live in areas of scrub and mesquite thickets. Length 8¾ inches

NORTHERN CARDINAL *Cardinalis cardinalis*

NOTHING CAN QUITE COMPARE with the brilliant red of this bird when seen against the newly fallen snow. No wonder it is featured on so many Christmas cards.

The song is loud and clear and most distinctive: *wheet, wheet wheet*, loud clear whistles with rising inflection, followed by a rapid series of *purtty purtty purtty–chew chew chew*. On the occasions when the female sings, the song can be almost as clear and ringing as the male's. The song can be delivered in any month but during the deep of winter is saved for sunny days when the warm rays reflect off the barn walls onto the thicket where it is wintering. Favored habitats are dense thickets and rose tangles.

It is such a beloved species that no fewer than seven states have chosen it as their state bird. For years it was always termed "the red bird of the south." In the 1950s it began to make its way northward and now has extended its range to the borders of Canada. It also appears to be slowly inching west so many more people will have the chance to enjoy this beautiful bird. The male in its vermillion colors with black mask and large bill set off with a distinct crest is unmistakable. The female is also quite beautiful in her own right. Warm brown buff with tints of red, reddish in the wings and tail and at the tip of the crest. The bill is a bright berry red that almost looks as if it had a berry embedded on it.

A permanent resident throughout its range it lends color and enjoyment to any trip afield at any time of the year.

♀

The all-red male cardinal is a welcome visitor to the garden not only for its beautiful coloration, but because it can break into song at any month of the year.

FACTS AND FEATURES

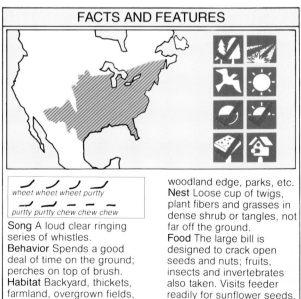

wheet wheet wheet purtty

purtty purtty chew chew chew

Song A loud clear ringing series of whistles.
Behavior Spends a good deal of time on the ground; perches on top of brush.
Habitat Backyard, thickets, farmland, overgrown fields, woodland edge, parks, etc.
Nest Loose cup of twigs, plant fibers and grasses in dense shrub or tangles, not far off the ground.
Food The large bill is designed to crack open seeds and nuts; fruits, insects and invertebrates also taken. Visits feeder readily for sunflower seeds.

The brilliant red color, the crest, the back, face and throat and the reddish conical bill make the cardinal an easily identifiable visitor to gardens offering water and berries. The female is less distinctive but can usually be identified by its bill which is similar to the male's. Cardinals are aggressive and can drive other birds away from a birdfeeder. Length up to 9 inches

A favorite of the backyard feeder, many people have asked "how can I increase my cardinal population?" One answer may be to try to broadcast your seed more. Each species of bird has an area that it will defend while feeding against the intrusion of a bird of the similar species. Some birds have a narrow feeding range (many of the blackbirds, for example), others need more room. The Cardinal is one. Therefore spreading sunflower seed in a limited area may attract only one pair. However, if scattered over a larger area several pairs may come to feed. There seems to be no lack of cardinals.

ROSE-BREASTED GROSBEAK *Pheucticus ludovicianus*

AS THE PINK OF CHERRY AND APPLE blossom tints the parkland and country lanes, the Rose-breasted Grosbeaks arrive. One of their favorite activities is to forage around these fruit trees and eat the ripening ovary of the flowers before they have a chance of setting into fruit. During this activity they sit practically motionless plucking all flowers within reach and manipulating them, allowing the pink petals to drift to the ground.

When they move into view, the males are really startling with a striking black hood and back running into the red glow of the breast patch and pure white underparts. The female by contrast looks more like a giant sparrow with warm browns, heavily streaked breast and broad head marking of white and brown stripes. Their bill is a massive cone designed for crushing the seeds of fruits. Even cherry pits are simple fare for such a massive structure.

In the mornings the male will take to the tree tops and there deliver his territorial serenade. A series of rich, clear notes, rapidly delivered. The call note is a diagnostic *chick* given throughout the year and in the fall is often the only giveaway of their presence in the multicolored foliage. The female bird sings on occasion, a harsh, short version of the male's tune. At times this will even be delivered while she is incubating the eggs. Although quite common, people think of the grosbeak as a rare species, as it is seldom seen during

FACTS AND FEATURES

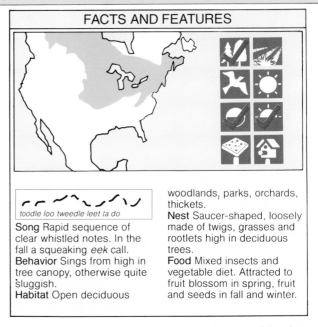

Song Rapid sequence of clear whistled notes. In the fall a squeaking *eek* call.
Behavior Sings from high in tree canopy, otherwise quite sluggish.
Habitat Open deciduous woodlands, parks, orchards, thickets.
Nest Saucer-shaped, loosely made of twigs, grasses and rootlets high in deciduous trees.
Food Mixed insects and vegetable diet. Attracted to fruit blossom in spring, fruit and seeds in fall and winter.

the breeding season because it spends most of the time high in the tree canopy. The nest, a very loose structure of sticks often so loosely assembled that one can see the eggs through it, is placed among the outer limbs high in the tree's crown.

Because it lives high in the treetops and is not often seen, this bird's sweet, robin-like song is the best indicator of its presence. In the fall, its squeaking eek *gives it away. A large bird with a massive seed-cracking bill, the male has a rose-colored throat patch and wing linings. Length 8 inches*

BLACK-HEADED GROSBEAK *Pheucticus melanocephalus*

♂

♀

The male black-headed grosbeak is distinguished by its black head, orange-brown throat and rump. Both sexes have a yellowish belly. During the breeding season the male bird utters his flight song in a wide semicircle above his territory. Length 7½ inches

IN THE SPRING when the Black-headed Grosbeak returns from its Mexican and Central American wintering grounds, woodlands, gardens, and streamsides of the West resound with the melodious whistling song. This bird has literally become the sign of spring in areas that show relatively little seasonal change – when the grosbeaks are back it is time for other species to start up their spring serenades.

Male Black-headed Grosbeaks are magnificent with their deep-orange cinnamon plumage, black-hooded head and wings of black flecked with white. The female, which occasionally sings though less melodiously than the male, is more like a giant sparrow with her bold white head streaks and a faint yellowish wash to the underparts. Looking at the female, one can see the close affinities with its eastern counterpart, the rose-breasted grosbeak. In fact, hybridization does sometimes take place in areas of overlapping range. Both species also tend to wander to the extremities of each other's range during aberrant migratory movements. The males are easy enough to separate; but in the females look for the yellow underwings of the black-headed form compared to the red underwings of the rose-breasted. Even the songs and squeaky *eeeak* notes are similar, which suggests that time and environment has acted to divide a large superspecies into two distinctive forms.

FACTS AND FEATURES

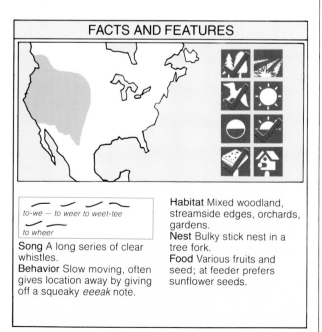

to-we — to weer to weet-tee
to wheer

Song A long series of clear whistles.
Behavior Slow moving, often gives location away by giving off a squeaky *eeeak* note.

Habitat Mixed woodland, streamside edges, orchards, gardens.
Nest Bulky stick nest in a tree fork.
Food Various fruits and seed; at feeder prefers sunflower seeds.

LAZULI BUNTING *Passerina amoena*

FACTS AND FEATURES

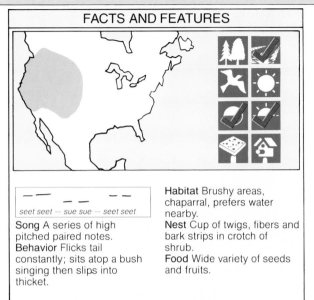

seet seet — sue sue -- seet seet

Song A series of high pitched paired notes.
Behavior Flicks tail constantly; sits atop a bush singing then slips into thicket.

Habitat Brushy areas, chaparral, prefers water nearby.
Nest Cup of twigs, fibers and bark strips in crotch of shrub.
Food Wide variety of seeds and fruits.

WHILE THE EAST has its dramatically blue indigo bunting, the West has its counterpart, the Lazuli Bunting – an all-American bird bedecked in the nation's colors of red, white and blue. And what striking colors: a back and head of turquoise, breast of orange-red and underbelly of pure white. Although it has a fairly wide range of habitats, brushy streamsides and thick scrub chaparral seem to be the favorites. From a brush top it delivers its rapid, jumbled song, not unlike that of the indigo bunting. In fact, in areas such as the Great Plains where the ranges of both the indigo and Lazuli overlap, hybrids have occurred. This has led many to say that the species should be lumped together as one. Others say that without consistent hybridization they remain separate species.

The female birds look remarkably similar, but the female Lazuli Bunting tends to have a bluish rump and the habit of flicking its tail, which aids identification. In earlier times this was a popular cage bird thanks to its brilliant colors and melodic song, and in Mexico they are still captured while on their wintering grounds. Fortunately, new international laws governing migrant birds have put a halt to much of the songbird trading worldwide.

In the southern part of its range, nesting can begin as early as March. The nest of twigs, fibers and bark strips is placed in a sturdy crotch of a shrub and if all goes well and food is plentiful, they may raise three broods.

With its bright blue head and throat, reddish sides and breast and white belly, the plumage of the male Lazuli bunting resembles that of the bluebird — but note the two wing bars and short stubby bill. This bird prefers open woodland with water nearby. Length 5½ inches

INDIGO BUNTING *Passerina cyanea*

A summer resident throughout much of the central and eastern states, the indigo bunting likes young plants in second-growth areas such as powerline clearings, orchards and parks. The male is deep blue but can look gray or black in poor light. The female is brown. Length 5½ inches

AS THE FIRST RAYS of morning sun warmed the massive stone temples of Mayan ruins on the Yucatan Peninsula of Mexico, a flock of small birds alighted in a dead tree projecting above the arid scrub. These were soon joined by other flocks that swirled up from the ground. With the early light all appeared black in color with obvious finch bills. Circling the tree to put the sun at my back the small black bodies came into full color – several hundred Indigo Buntings. The deep indigo blue is the result of feather structure and refraction of light and there is no blue pigment in the feathers. Therefore, as the birds moved about the blue appeared to twinkle as it went from total indigo to black or gray. These birds were massing for their journey back to North America for nesting.

By early May they would be dotted across the eastern half of the country in every overgrown field, orchard or secondary growth land. They announce their presence by a loud song given in short bursts of paired high pitched phrases. A constant singer, once on territory they sing on through even the hottest hours of midday. The nest is placed in a thicket usually not very high off the ground. A cup of grasses and rootlets, it is often parasitized by brown-headed cowbirds that sit and watch until the nest is left unattended, then slip in to deposit their egg. It is not a rare sight to see an Indigo Bunting labor to feed a massive young cowbird. By late summer the male begins to take on the mottled plumage of the winter adult: brownish in color with splotchings of blue. The female is a dull brown and lacks streaks. The male will hold out well into August

before reluctantly terminating his singing, which makes it one of the latest singing species on the continent. As they retreat south, thickets, garden plots and weedy fields of agricultural land are scoured for seeds. As a great deal of land has been left to go fallow with the diminution of small-time farm operations, the Indigo Bunting is profiting from the increased habitat, with the result that their range is expanding rapidly to both the South and West.

FACTS AND FEATURES

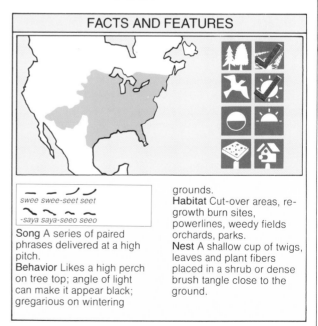

swee swee-seet seet

-saya saya-seeo seeo

Song A series of paired phrases delivered at a high pitch.
Behavior Likes a high perch on tree top; angle of light can make it appear black; gregarious on wintering grounds.
Habitat Cut-over areas, re-growth burn sites, powerlines, weedy fields orchards, parks.
Nest A shallow cup of twigs, leaves and plant fibers placed in a shrub or dense brush tangle close to the ground.

DICKCISSEL *Spiza americana*

In midwestern prairies, these birds appear to sit on every fence and powerline. They resemble house sparrows in shape and movement, but their broad malar stripes help set them apart. The male also has a rich yellow belly and black bib. Length 6-7 inches

GREGARIOUS is certainly one word that sums up the Dickcissel. In all aspects of its life it is usually found with others of its kind or with similar species. It is a species that inhabits rank weedy meadows and fields of the Midwest. The male is polygamous and therefore nesting is in loose colonies. The females build the small cup of grasses directly on the ground in among grass and shrub bases or, rarely, up off the ground in the base of a shrub or on a grass clump. Large fields may have several such colonies so one is virtually inundated with Dickcissels in such situations.

The males sing from atop bushes, grass clumps, wire fences and power lines. While driving through this grassland area during breeding season it seems as if there is a male Dickcissel on the wires or fences between every pole. The bird's name is derived from the call of the male, *see see–Dick, Dick–cissel, cissel*. In breeding plumage the male looks like a tiny meadowlark, brown with rich rusty shoulders and yellow on the face and around the eye and chest. The chest also sports the black throat mark reminiscent of the meadowlark. The females and immatures look very like house sparrows with white throat and reddish shoulders.

Although the majority of the birds winter from Mexico on through Central America, a number of birds show up at feeders on the East Coast. There they blend in with the house sparrow flocks feeding on seeds. A quick glance and they can be overlooked but with

quick glance and they can be overlooked but with consistent searching of sparrow flocks your diligence will be rewarded. On the winter grounds the birds mass by the thousands. Agricultural lands are a prime choice, as are stock-feeding yards. In Costa Rica I have seen flocks in rice fields that we estimated to be in excess of a quarter of a million birds!

FACTS AND FEATURES

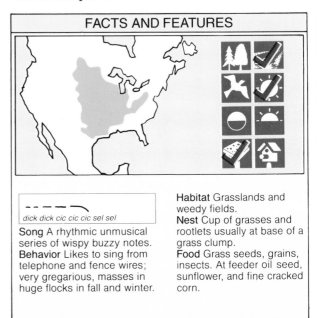

dick dick cic cic cic sel sel

Song A rhythmic unmusical series of wispy buzzy notes.
Behavior Likes to sing from telephone and fence wires; very gregarious, masses in huge flocks in fall and winter.

Habitat Grasslands and weedy fields.
Nest Cup of grasses and rootlets usually at base of a grass clump.
Food Grass seeds, grains, insects. At feeder oil seed, sunflower, and fine cracked corn.

GREEN-TAILED TOWHEE *Pipilo chlorurus*

FACTS AND FEATURES

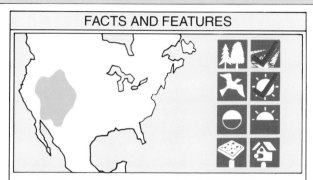

sweet-oooo

Song Opens with a clear, whistled *sweet-oooo* followed by a series of jumbled notes with a raspy central portion.
Behavior Secretive, often runs rather than flies into cover; scratches with both feet.
Habitat Dense shrubs of high plateau country.
Nest Large cup of grasses and bark shreds situated in dense shrub.
Food Wide variety of seeds and fruits, also some insects.

ONE ENCOUNTERS this handsome species in dense shrubbery, in the high plateau country of the West. Once located, the Green-tailed Towhee is secretive and will usually run quickly for cover and dart out of sight.

However, inquisitiveness seems to overcome its initial fear for the birds generally work their way back out into the open, often sitting in full view. The white throat is the giveaway and looks as though a cotton ball had been tucked under the bird's chin. The top of the head is a rich rusty color, the back greenish-olive and the underparts gray. As with all sparrows, the young birds are heavily streaked which gives one a clue as to its identification, but the white chin and white line below the eye will clinch it.

If heard first it has a call note much like the mew of a catbird. In addition, its double-foot scratching, typical of all towhees, will surely catch one's ear as the bird forages in the underbrush. The song is a rich outpouring of notes with a harsh raspy portion interjected into the middle of the sequence. The introductory notes *sweet-ooooo* clearly whistled lead one to believe they are hearing a fox sparrow until the songster is sighted.

In the winter there is a strong southerly movement, and at this time they seem to be attracted to foraging with flocks of white-crowned sparrows. They are great wanderers from their normal migration route, and many easterners have added this species to their life list as they invariably show up at feeders and become a real winter prize.

This is the only towhee with green on its back. It is a shy bird that scratches under scrub for food and lives in chaparral and underbrush at high elevations. Length 7 inches

RUFOUS-SIDED TOWHEE *Pipilo erythrophthalmus*

FACTS AND FEATURES

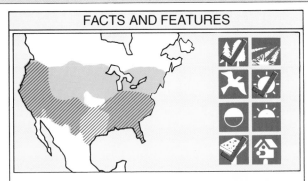

chewink/drink your tea

Song A distinct call, and a loud clear song with the ending drawn out.
Behavior Very inquisitive; spreads tail as it hops about; scratches noisily with both feet at once among dead leaves.
Habitat Dry woods, and riverside thickets, weedy hillsides, chaparral, parks.
Nest Leaves, bark strips and twigs, lined with fine grasses or pine needles, tucked into a depression on the ground under cover of shrubs.

MANY A BEGINNING BIRDER has been introduced to this large handsome sparrow on their first walk into an upland woodland or scrub filled valley when the leader has pointed out: "Listen, hear that distant song – *drink–your–tea*." Once heard it is not forgotten. Neither is the call that gives the bird its name – *towheee* – or one of its often-used vernacular names – *chewink*!

It is a common bird of a wide variety of habitats from coast to coast and north to the Canadian border. There are many different races, be it the plain black-backed eastern form or the distinctive spotted and striped backed western form. Very often while birding the birds can be heard scratching in the leaf litter. If seen they will be making a very quick move with both their feet at once raking out leaves with a double kick action. (Kicking both feet backwards isn't an easy trick but several species of birds have evolved this action.) Seeds and insects form a principal part of their diet.

The Rufous-sided Towhee is a large sparrow with long tail. The male has a distinctive black back and hood (spotted back in western form) and has rich rufous chestnut sides. The underbelly is white. The female, who sings only on rare occasions, is brown on the head and back where the male is black.

Note: the western forms do not give the *drink–your–tea* call. It is replaced here by a slurred *ju–eeee*.

A sparrow with a long tail, this towhee lives in parks, gardens, woods and scrubland of all kinds throughout much of the western and southern states, and its range is growing northward. It rakes the ground under cover with both of its feet to expose seeds. Length 8 inches

Bachman's Sparrow *Aimophila aestivalis*

ON A COOL SPRING MORNING when a trace of fog slowly lifts from the dense palmetto stand that blankets the pinewoods floor comes a sweet two-part song, somewhat reminiscent of the liquid notes of a hermit thrush. Scanning the dead branches that protrude above the palmetto one encounters a rather drab looking sparrow sitting with a vertical posture. It throws its head back and out pours the sweet cascade of notes. This is the pinewoods sparrow of old terminology in its perfect setting.

In the northern parts of its range it favors abandoned fields and thicketed edges. Within this northern area it seems to be slowly disappearing and retracting to its southern haunts. The reason for this is not totally clear. Certainly it is the pine belt of the South that one envisions as the prime haunt of this species. Though its song is diagnostic, getting a good glimpse of this bird is not always easy. It seems reluctant to sit in the open for any duration of time, and more often than not will pop up into view for a moment before twisting off in flight and diving back into the dense undercover.

When it is seen it is not too impressive. Reddish-brown on the back with warm buff underparts showing a hint of streaking, the back is lined with gray and the crown is striped with rust and gray alternating lines. Finding its nest is a major project and often made impossible by the sharp palmetto fronds at whose base it is usually placed. In addition one must beware as the palmetto scrub is ideal rattlesnake country. However, if all these barriers are surpassed and luck brings you to

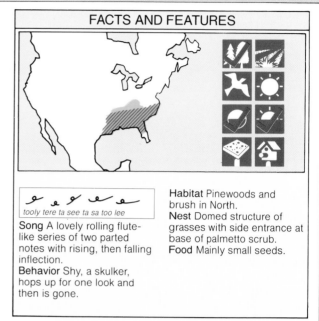

FACTS AND FEATURES

tooly tere ta see ta sa too lee

Song A lovely rolling flute-like series of two parted notes with rising, then falling inflection.
Behavior Shy, a skulker, hops up for one look and then is gone.

Habitat Pinewoods and brush in North.
Nest Domed structure of grasses with side entrance at base of palmetto scrub.
Food Mainly small seeds.

a nest, it will be found to be a tight-domed structure made of plant fibers and grasses and with a discreet side entrance.

This species was named for the Reverend John Bachman, a close friend of Audubon's when the famous painter was working in the South on his *Birds of America*.

*Similar to the field sparrow but with a darker bill and dark tail, the Bachman's sparrow has a gray back streaked with dark brown, light gray underparts and a white belly. A western subspecies has dark chestnut brown plumage above and tan below. This sparrow lives in dry areas with scattered trees.
Length 6 inches*

TREE SPARROW *Spizella arborea*

This sparrow spends the winter across much of the northern half of the country. It sings its sweet, rich song in the early spring just before it departs for its far north breeding ground. The largest of the rust-capped sparrows, it has plain gray underparts, an orange-chestnut back streaked with white and black and a black "stickpin" mark on its chest. Length 6 inches

FOR THE BIRDER who lives outside of Canada or Alaska this is a bird that is a true winter visitor. In a good portion of the lower 48 states it arrives with the cold, crisp nights of the October harvest moon. Weedy fields, brush piles and marsh edges are usual first selected sites, where the bird's sweet *see–it* or *tweedle–it* call gives its presence away. When it hops into view it is quite easy to identify with its fox-red crown, two-tone black and yellow bill and the distinct black "stick-pin" spot on the clear gray breast. As winter sets in they usually move from these foraging areas into more suburban sites and become common residents in and above the bird-feeding trays. Gathering up a wide variety of seed types they do not seem particular in their food choices although sunflower seed is a favorite for all the finches.

The birds will linger on into the onset of spring and by the end of April most are well along on their route back north. This deprives us of one of the finer types of songs given by the sparrow groups. Occasionally they will sing and certainly on their northern breeding grounds it is one of the commonest songs to be heard at the tree line. Introduced by clear *sweet sweet sweet* notes, a series of fluid warbling notes follow. The song is repeated over and over again. These birds nest north of the tree line and beyond out into the low thicketed valleys of the tundra. The nest, placed on the ground, is a cup of grasses and sedges lined with rootlets, finer

grasses and feathers, often from the ptarmigan – they live in the area and are in molt at this time of nesting. And so it is that the valleys ring with their sweet music until it is time to head south again and bring pleasure to feeder watchers across the country.

FACTS AND FEATURES

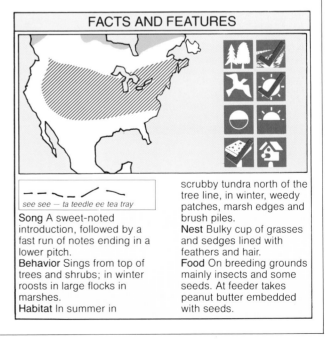

see see — ta teedle ee tea tray

Song A sweet-noted introduction, followed by a fast run of notes ending in a lower pitch.
Behavior Sings from top of trees and shrubs; in winter roosts in large flocks in marshes.
Habitat In summer in scrubby tundra north of the tree line, in winter, weedy patches, marsh edges and brush piles.
Nest Bulky cup of grasses and sedges lined with feathers and hair.
Food On breeding grounds mainly insects and some seeds. At feeder takes peanut butter embedded with seeds.

CHIPPING SPARROW *Spizella passerina*

TO THE EASTERNER, the "Chippy" has become the familiar bird of the backyard, garden or field edge. For the Westerner it is a species that does visit orchards but seems to prefer life in the evergreen forests. At campsites in the western mountains the "Chippy" is often seen hopping along the roadsides and shuffling about in the pine needles. This dual life means that this little bird is highly adaptive and therefore is found throughout most of the United States. Its trim form, brown back and gray underparts, a chestnut cap, black line through the eye with distinct white line over it, and small black bill make this one of the easiest sparrows to identify.

Its song has given this bird its name: a long progression of dry rattle-like *chipps* given on one basic scale. Studies have shown that what to our ears sound like similar songs if slowed down via special tape recording methods prove to be very distinctive in their delivery. Hence, when one stands in a cemetery (a favored habitat in the East) and listens to several of these birds singing from various evergreens, though the songs sound basically the same to us, each male can differentiate them and is thus well aware of the other bird's territory.

The nest is a dainty cup-like structure of coarse grasses and rootlets lined with animal hair. In the past horsehair was the prime nest lining but with the disappearance of the horse from towns and cities, dog,

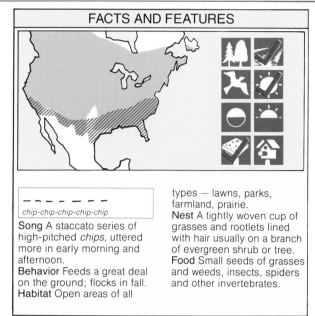

FACTS AND FEATURES

---
chip-chip-chip-chip-chip

Song A staccato series of high-pitched *chips*, uttered more in early morning and afternoon.
Behavior Feeds a great deal on the ground; flocks in fall.
Habitat Open areas of all types — lawns, parks, farmland, prairie.
Nest A tightly woven cup of grasses and rootlets lined with hair usually on a branch of evergreen shrub or tree.
Food Small seeds of grasses and weeds, insects, spiders and other invertebrates.

cat and squirrel hairs seem to be new substitutes.

In the northern part of its range these sparrows migrate south for the winter, and in October when autumn colors tint the land, large bands of "Chippies" mass at field edges and on lawns signaling that winter is drawing near.

A familiar sight shuttling along the ground in search of grass seed or building material, this sparrow is easy to identify because of its brick-red cap, light gray line over the eye and black line running from the bill through the eye to the nape of the neck. Its call is a prolonged staccato. Length 5½ inches

LARK BUNTING *Calamospiza melanocorys*

THIS IS THE SONGBIRD of sagebrush and dry prairie regions. A vist to such dry open areas is sure to reward the birder with views of the handsome males, all black in color and with brilliant white wing patches, as they take flight and sail about on stiffened wings in courtship flight over their territory. This territory is not really strongly defended, so many males may be seen in a fairly small section of prairie. As with many other birds of open regions, lack of perch availability for song means they have taken to the air to proclaim their springtime feelings. The song is a spirited outpouring of notes, although more commonly heard in migration is a distinct *who–lee* note.

The female is a streaky sparrow-like color with the distinctive white patch in its wing, although not as pronounced as in the male. Certainly one standout feature of this species is the very large bill. These birds feed on the ground and are fond of all types of seeds and many insects, especially grasshoppers. The nest is placed on the ground and is made from grasses.

In winter massive flocks build up and often intersperse with plains longspur flocks in the South, especially Texas. There, in feed lots and short grain fields hundreds and hundreds are not uncommon. In addition a few representatives wander to the East and West

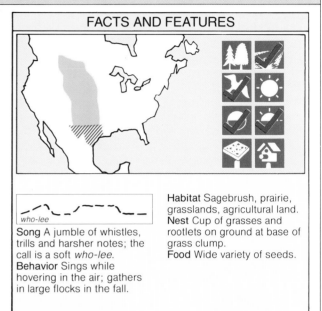

FACTS AND FEATURES

who-lee

Song A jumble of whistles, trills and harsher notes; the call is a soft *who-lee*.
Behavior Sings while hovering in the air; gathers in large flocks in the fall.

Habitat Sagebrush, prairie, grasslands, agricultural land.
Nest Cup of grasses and rootlets on ground at base of grass clump.
Food Wide variety of seeds.

Coasts each year, adding spark to a day spent afield looking at sparrows!

The male lark bunting resembles the bobolink but has a white patch on its wings rather than on its back. It also has white tips on its tail feathers and a large thick gray bill. The female is streaked and has small tan wing patches. Lark buntings prefer dry areas and live in sagebrush and short prairie grass. Length 7 inches

HENSLOW'S SPARROW *Ammodramus henslowii*

A rare bird, the Henslow's sparrow lives in damp fields and meadows with plenty of weeds. It differs from all other sparrows in its combination of streaked breast, olive nape and hind crown, and chestnut-brown wings. Its back is heavily streaked, its underparts are white with tan on the flanks and its breast is streaked with black. Length 5 inches.

WHEN ONE GETS TO KNOW the Henslow's Sparrow, and that is no easy task, it is hard to believe that it is classed as a songbird at all. It is said to have the shortest song of any of the songbirds – a sharp, short insect-like *tis–lick*. Though they do sing in the daytime, the low light intensity of evening seems to initiate their main singing period. To add to the confusion, this is also the singing time for many crickets with a similar song. So, here we have a true test for the bird-song *aficionado* – to pick out the Henslow's Sparrow from a field of crickets at night. Both bird and insect will sing on and on during still spring and summer nights. As Roger Tory Peterson has said, "it's such a poor singer perhaps it needs more time to practice!"

A resident of the shrubby weedy meadows and fields of the northeast and central states, its choice of nesting areas is quite spotty. What may seem like a perfect habitat is often vacant! The populations may move from one site to another, use it for several years and then disappear for a time before reusing it or simply disappear for good. Totally unpredictable is the best description of its breeding habits. Obviously it must have very specific needs for occupancy, and these needs are not always apparent to the birder. Also when on site they act like mice rather than birds. In several instances I have closed in on this species to have them literally escape running between my legs or over my feet. If flushed they fly for only a short distance before diving back into the grasses. On rare occasions they will sit up in view for just a short period.

It is a stocky sparrow with an overly-large flat-topped head of a deep olive drab color. The back is rusty with streaking and the buff chest is streaked. The wings are very rusty in color.

FACTS AND FEATURES

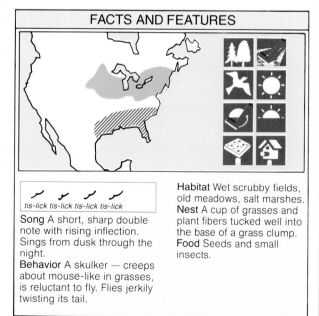

tis-lick tis-lick tis-lick tis-lick

Song A short, sharp double note with rising inflection. Sings from dusk through the night.
Behavior A skulker — creeps about mouse-like in grasses, is reluctant to fly. Flies jerkily twisting its tail.

Habitat Wet scrubby fields, old meadows, salt marshes.
Nest A cup of grasses and plant fibers tucked well into the base of a grass clump.
Food Seeds and small insects.

133

FOX SPARROW *Passerella iliaca*

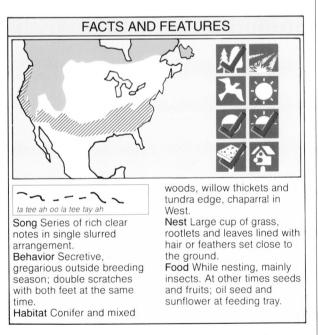

This bird breeds in the far north, and its loud, sweet song is seldom heard except in its breeding grounds. The bird varies widely in color and pattern, but most have heavy markings on the underparts merging into a spot on the upper breast and are reddish brown to gray-brown above. Length 7 inches

FOR A GOOD PORTION of the United States this is a winter feeder bird. When it does arrive its size and fox-like color certainly make it stand out against the white blanket of snow that drives it into the feeders from nearby thicket and weed fields. At 7in, it is not only one of our largest sparrows but one of the handsomest. There are many subspecies, however, and in coloration the bird can be the bright rust that gives the species its name or dark chocolate brown as seen in the Pacific Northwest forms. The one feature that is consistent is the rusty tail. When scratching about in thickets, which they do with a double foot kick method, the first appearance can lead one to think of a hermit thrush. However, the bill immediately eliminates that species. The large bill of the sparrow is designed for feeding on seeds and fruits and much of their winter movement is based on the availability of these items.

The Fox Sparrow could also rank as the sweetest singer among sparrows. In the alder thickets of Alaskan tundra swales the sweet, bubbly song punctuates crisp spring mornings. The birds can be quite shy and quickly slip from their shrub-top perch at the first sign of an intruder. The more open the area inhabited, the shyer the birds, so one must take quick advantage of any available sparse cover. The West Coast birds are often encountered as they scratch about the paths through the coastal brush and chaparral. On quiet

FACTS AND FEATURES

ta tee ah oo la tee tay ah

Song Series of rich clear notes in single slurred arrangement.
Behavior Secretive, gregarious outside breeding season; double scratches with both feet at the same time.
Habitat Conifer and mixed woods, willow thickets and tundra edge, chaparral in West.
Nest Large cup of grass, rootlets and leaves lined with hair or feathers set close to the ground.
Food While nesting, mainly insects. At other times seeds and fruits; oil seed and sunflower at feeding tray.

mornings such scratching in dry leaves can lead you to expect a massive animal soon looming into view, only to have this sparrow pop out and flutter off giving a loud *chick* note and a vision of fleeting rust!

VESPER SPARROW *Pooecetes gramineus*

IN EARLY TIMES known as bay-winged bunting and spectacled bunting, these two names point out two key features of the bird we know as the Vesper Sparrow. The rusty bay patch of the wing is often conspicuous, and the large white eye ring certainly is. In addition, when flushed the outer tail feathers flash white.

The term "vesper" was coined because those who heard its song felt that the evening was the best time to appreciate it. In fact, the species sings throughout the day, and happens to have one of the more charming songs of all the sparrows. It is a clear whistled series that begins with distinct phrases which then rapidly trails off. There are many interpretations but the basic pattern is *tear–tear, tore–tore–here–we–go–down–the–hill*. These songs are usually delivered from perches higher than the normal grass clump top – low tree branches at field edges, or fence posts.

The nest is a loose cup of grasses tucked into the base of a grass clump. More often than not it is found when the birder nearly steps on it and is startled as the occupant flushes up from his feet and flashes its outer tail feathers. It has rather catholic choice of habitats – sand plains, low grass areas, prairies, beach-grasses, barrens, etc – which unfortunately represent waste areas ripe for use to the land developer. This is one of the reasons the Vesper Sparrow is disappearing over many places within its range, especially in the East.

FACTS AND FEATURES

tear-tear tore-tore-here-we-go-down-the hill

Song A progression of two phrase sequences that scale downward in rapid succession.
Behavior Alert, often sings from a fence post or low tree limb at clearing edge.

Habitat Open areas — grasslands, sand and gravel pits.
Nest Of grasses and plant fibers on ground.
Food Grass seeds, berries.

Often seen in meadows, fields and prairies, the vesper sparrow can be distinguished from other sparrows by its short notched tail with white outer feathers, the chesnut brown on its wing and its white eye ring. It also has dark cheek patches and two inconspicuous wing bars. Length 6 inches

SONG SPARROW *Melospiza melodia*

A year-round resident in most parts of the country, the song sparrow is much admired for its song. This consists of a series of three seet, seet, seet *notes followed by a bubbling trill. It lives in thickets, hedges and brush and will visit low birdfeeders or eat seed scattered on the ground.*
Length 5½-7 inches

THE SONG SPARROW makes its home in thickets and dense scrub from coast to coast and throughout most of Canada. It is a bird of the backyard, the park and the woodland edge. Fortunately it has a lovely song and it is fairly easy to learn. Three or four clear introductory notes are followed by a rolling series of sweet notes ending in a buzzy trill. To Northerners, the trial songs of spring which seem unperfected when first heard announce winter's disappearance. By the time the song has reached its full sound spring is back and the harbinger has been right again!

It is a long-tailed sparrow and when seen fleetingly as it disappears into a shrub or wood pile, the elongated tail seems to spiral into the air just as it slips out of sight. When perched atop a stub or favored dead snag with head thrown back and in full song it is seen to best advantage – grayish face with rich chestnut head stripes, chestnut back and heavily streaked chest and sides of dark brown. A concentration of two small and one large chest spots merge at a distance to give the identifying "stickpin" field mark.

The species is highly variable. Some 30 sub-species are represented in North America, ranging from the large dark form of the Aleutian Islands of Alaska to the pale forms of the southwestern deserts. Therefore one should note where they will spend time birding and be aware of the differences of one of the commonest birds that could go unidentified for a few days because of its variability. It should also be noted that for some reason the species is missing from the southern tip of Texas and Florida!

Another interesting note is the variation in nest site choices. Earlier nesting birds almost always place the cup of grasses, wet stems, bark and rootlets directly on the ground beneath a sheltering shrub or low-growing plant. The birds nesting later in the season tend to be more low-tree and shrub nesters. At the nest both parents tend the young and often the male is still on young-raising duty when the female is off sitting on the second set of eggs for the season. With that work regime it is no wonder that the Song Sparrows are one of our most abundant songbirds.

FACTS AND FEATURES

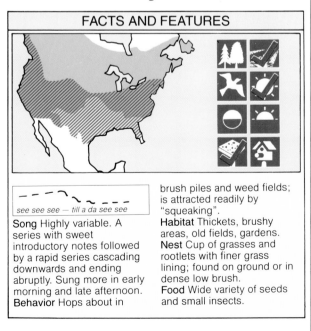

see see see — till a da see see

Song Highly variable. A series with sweet introductory notes followed by a rapid series cascading downwards and ending abruptly. Sung more in early morning and late afternoon.
Behavior Hops about in brush piles and weed fields; is attracted readily by "squeaking".
Habitat Thickets, brushy areas, old fields, gardens.
Nest Cup of grasses and rootlets with finer grass lining; found on ground or in dense low brush.
Food Wide variety of seeds and small insects.

136

WHITE–THROATED SPARROW *Zonotrichia albicollis*

FACTS AND FEATURES

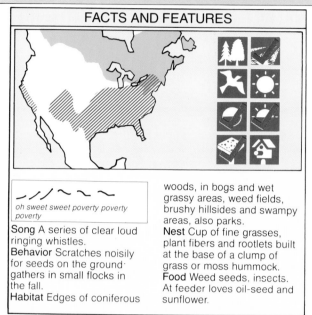

~ / / ~ ~ ~

oh sweet sweet poverty poverty poverty

Song A series of clear loud ringing whistles.
Behavior Scratches noisily for seeds on the ground· gathers in small flocks in the fall.
Habitat Edges of coniferous

woods, in bogs and wet grassy areas, weed fields, brushy hillsides and swampy areas, also parks.
Nest Cup of fine grasses, plant fibers and rootlets built at the base of a clump of grass or moss hummock.
Food Weed seeds. insects. At feeder loves oil-seed and sunflower.

IF ONE WERE TO ASK a group of people to compile a list of their backyard feeder birds, this bird would occur within the top 10 or perhaps five. It is a classic feeding-station bird. They occur in large numbers, are easy to identify and will stay in or near a yard for an entire winter if the feeding sequence is on a set regime. They are fascinating to watch scratching for food as they kick out material with both feet at the same time. What would seem to be a move that would lead to falling is timed perfectly and disaster avoided.

They are large handsome sparrows. Rich brown rust on the back with distinctive white and black head stripes. The throat is pure white in adults and dusky gray on the immatures. Note the area between the eye and the base of the bill called the lores. In top plumage this is a rich lemon yellow. Their nesting areas lie mainly in Canada and the boglands of New England and the Appalachians in the evergreen zone. It is on their breeding grounds that the sweet diagnostic song is best heard. It is a long, drawn out but melodic *oh sweet-sweet-poverty-poverty-poverty*. The song varies depending on what part of its range you are in. On migration and on its wintering grounds it inhabits thickets and understory of woodlands. In this situation the best note to listen for is the sweet *tseep* note, usually an indicator that a foraging flock is near.

Note: This species is polymorphic ie it has two color phases. In one, the head streaks are pure white and in the other they are buff. Check to see which comes to your feeder next fall.

The scratching of leaves or the loud ringing, oh sweet, sweet sweet *is usually the first indication of the presence of this sparrow. A large, handsome bird with a black and white striped head and a pure white throat, it lives in deep coniferous forests or bogs and eats seeds. Length 7 inches*

WHITE-CROWNED SPARROW *Zonotrichia leucophrys*

A winter resident to much of the country, this bird moves to its nesting ground in the far north during the summer. In winter, it lives in both open areas and thickets and comes readily to a birdfeeder for seeds and water. Length up to 7 inches

WITH ITS BLACK CAP and white stripes jauntily tilted forward, large size and the grayness of its body, an adult White-crowned Sparrow is a striking bird and one of the commonest species of the West Coast and sub-Arctic North. One of the true heralds of spring in the open tundra, the woodsman who has endured the long, cold, dark winter awaits that first song delivered from a shrub nearby sometime in early May. Other arrivals soon follow and the forest edge and tundra swale is quickly alive with the sound of the clear introduction notes followed by a rapid run of twittering down-slurred trills. The birds seem to be atop every small snag and continue to call all through the long sub-Arctic days.

Farther south along the West Coast the same song is heard off and on throughout the year, but begins in earnest in the early spring. Here, the White-crowned Sparrow is also a common species of weedy thickets, brushy areas, parklands and gardens. Every roadside pullout along the rugged California coast will have its share of White-crowns hopping out to pick up any dropped crumb.

Still, in many areas this species remains a bit reclusive. It will work its way through a thicket, peer at the intruder for a moment and then slip off into the brush, often proving difficult to relocate. The nest, a cup of grasses, is tucked well into dense ground vegetation. Along these lines a maintained brush pile at a garden's edge can often attract a nesting pair of these

most handsome sparrows.

For the Easterner it is a bird of passage headed for more southerly wintering grounds. The majority of the migration south is through the Great Plains and mid-Atlantic States, so the bird remains uncommon in the Northeast. Sightings are predominantly of young birds with rusty crown stripes.

FACTS AND FEATURES

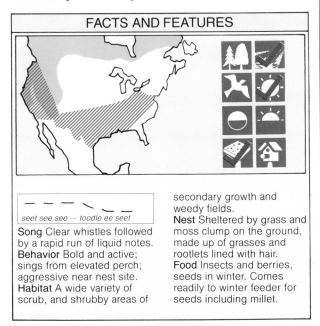

seet see see — toodle ee seet

Song Clear whistles followed by a rapid run of liquid notes.
Behavior Bold and active; sings from elevated perch; aggressive near nest site.
Habitat A wide variety of scrub, and shrubby areas of secondary growth and weedy fields.
Nest Sheltered by grass and moss clump on the ground, made up of grasses and rootlets lined with hair.
Food Insects and berries, seeds in winter. Comes readily to winter feeder for seeds including millet.

DARK-EYED JUNCO *Junco hyemalis*

FOR MOST OF THE EASTERN SEABOARD and the South the Dark-eyed Junco arrives with the first cold blasts of northern winds in the fall. Among the colorful leaves of roadsides small parties of these birds flush up into the trees as cars pass. The white edging to the tail is diagnostic enough to make the identification. In fields and woodland edges they mingle with mixed groupings of sparrow relatives as they forage for seeds often calling in concert, with a varied warble–twitter, or odd *clunk* or *smack* sounds. With the first heavy snows the Juncos wend their way to the more easily obtained food of backyard feeding stations. They are principally ground feeders and are usually quite reluctant to go up to a feeding tray so seeds should be tossed in snow-cleared areas. They will then shuffle about as they crouch close to the ground adding warmth to their feet as they feed on sunflower and other smaller seeds.

The Dark-eyed Junco is a denizen of northern spruce forests but also nests in open blueberry pastures among piles of slash pine from lumber camps. The song is a simple musical trill, similar to that of a chipping sparrow.

The nest is a nicely woven cup placed on the ground, usually under a slight overhang. The young are very sparrow-like, being heavily streaked and brown, but do have the white outer tail feathers. During migration or on wintering grounds you can expect this familiar bird in a very wide range of habitats.

This species has gone through a remarkable number of name changes and shows dramatic color changes depending on the geographical location of the population. The West is dominated by the "Oregon form" with rusty back and contrasting black hood. There is the "gray-headed form" of Arizona and Mexico with its rusty back; and the isolated Black Hills of South Dakota are the habitat for the "white-winged form." In the East the old name of "slate-colored" still holds sway with many birders but technically all the above forms are lumped in "Dark-eyed Junco."

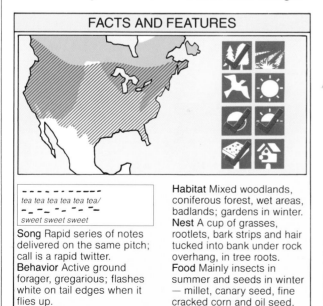

FACTS AND FEATURES

---
tea tea tea tea tea tea/

sweet sweet sweet

Song Rapid series of notes delivered on the same pitch; call is a rapid twitter.
Behavior Active ground forager, gregarious; flashes white on tail edges when it flies up.

Habitat Mixed woodlands, coniferous forest, wet areas, badlands; gardens in winter.
Nest A cup of grasses, rootlets, bark strips and hair tucked into bank under rock overhang, in tree roots.
Food Mainly insects in summer and seeds in winter — millet, canary seed, fine cracked corn and oil seed.

Once several species, this bird is now recognized as one species with different forms. All forms have a pink bill, white outer tail feathers, white underparts and dark eyes, and they all share a long, slow monotonous trill. Length 5½ inches

HOUSE FINCH *Carpodacus mexicanus*

DURING THE 1960s one of the most asked questions at lectures was: "What is this purple finch-like bird that is coming to my feeder?" The bird was the House Finch and the reason no bird book had it pictured for the East was that from its introduction to Long Island in the 1940s until the late 1950s the population was still only small. However, since the late 1950s the population has boomed. Flocks began showing up and many were incorrectly identified as purple finches, but the House Finch is not as bulky a bird. Also, the rose-red is brighter (orange in western forms and scattered eastern birds) and is confined to the breast, eyeline and rump. The rest of the bird is brownish and with distinct brown streaks on the sides, flanks and underbelly. The female is similar to the purple finch but has less distinct streaking.

The House Finch has also become one of the favorite songsters. On warm mornings, even in winter, their sweet rapid jumble of notes cascading from an ivy-covered wall is enough to cheer up anyone.

At the feeder this species has become one of the dominant members of the morning visitors. It is aggressive and loves sunflower seeds. Its aggression towards house sparrows has endeared them to many and in some areas it has forced these birds out.

Of course all this is familiar to the birders of the West Coast. An abundant, permanent resident there, it can

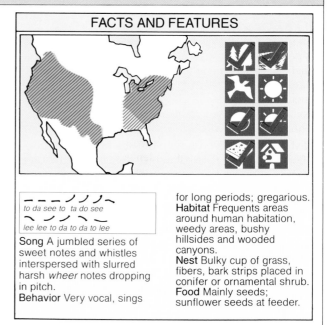

FACTS AND FEATURES

to da see to ta do see

lee lee to da to da to lee

Song A jumbled series of sweet notes and whistles interspersed with slurred harsh *wheer* notes dropping in pitch.
Behavior Very vocal, sings for long periods; gregarious.
Habitat Frequents areas around human habitation, weedy areas, bushy hillsides and wooded canyons.
Nest Bulky cup of grass, fibers, bark strips placed in conifer or ornamental shrub.
Food Mainly seeds; sunflower seeds at feeder.

be found in nearly every type of habitat.

With its aggressive ways and ability to feed on many types of seeds, co-exist with man and adapt to many environmental areas the success of the eastern population meeting with the west seems inevitable.

*The house finch, like the purple finch, is rosy red in color, but its red is confined to the forehead, breast and rump. It prefers to live near humans and sometimes spends its entire life in one area rewarding its neighbors with a beautiful, bubbling song.
Length 6 inches*

♀

♂

AMERICAN GOLDFINCH *Carduelis tristis*

"THE GOLDFINCHES ARE BACK and cleaning out my thistle feeders." The cry of the winter feeding station attendant. But what better bird to have visit! In the winter months, cloaked in drab olives with black wings that sport white barring, they cling to the feeders and hang in every which way as they split the seeds with their conical bills. As spring approaches the yellow color slowly starts to show as plumages wear. (Wear plumage is not common in the bird world but this species is a fine example of the process.) By spring they are back in their brilliant golden garb and wandering about in loose flocks. Trees often come alive with the sweet twittering songs of numerous males. In all cases a distinctive *swee* note in a rising inflection can be heard identifying the songster. Though at their finest during the spring, nesting is often postponed until well into the summer because fine thistledown is a favorite addition to the newly completed nest. The nest is a solid structure placed in the fork of a tree branch and made of plant fibers, cotton and wool-like in their texture, and with spider and caterpillar nest webbing. All this gives the nest a gray appearance.

Resident throughout much of their range, after nesting they group together to look for feeding stations loaded with seed. Once one has been located the distinct *perch–a–week* of the birds in flight can be heard and the group's roller-coasting flight pattern detected as they swirl down from the sky and literally cover the feeder. A lot of seed will be used from then on, as well as old sunflower heads placed out or left standing in the garden plot.

FACTS AND FEATURES

perch-a-week

Song The flight song is perhaps the best known, a three-parted *perch-a-week*. Otherwise song is a jumble of sweet whistles and twitterings.
Behavior Lively, moves about in groups. Has roller-coaster type flight, utters flight note at top of rise.
Habitat Open fields, weedy areas, roadsides, farmlands, gardens.
Nest A beautiful cup of grasses and plant fibers in the fork of a shrub, lined with thistle down.
Food Mainly seeds but insects taken during nesting.

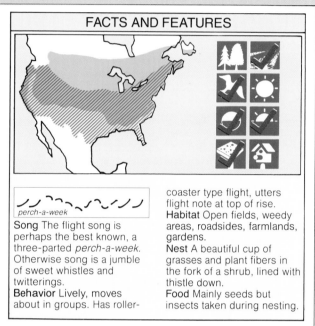

The male goldfinch is brilliant yellow with a black cap which turns brownish gray in winter. It eats seed, especially of thistle, but reinforces this plant diet with insects during the breeding season. Length 5 inches

RED CROSSBILL *Loxia curvirostra*

IN LUSH MOUNTAIN FOREST with extensive hillsides of evergreens and the warmth of being south of the border, I roamed the Mexican mountains in quest of birdlife. Suddenly high above drifted down a familiar sound. But could it be – Red Crossbills in Mexico? They swung in and came to rest in the top of the pine. Putting my glasses on I could see their unique crossed mandibles, used for opening evergreen cones. Many would have the same feeling, that the Red Crossbill is a northern species. But looking at its full range one can see that it lives throughout the high areas of the West right the way down through the Mexican mountains. Indeed, there is even a relic population in the mountains of Haiti!

These Crossbills are very irregular in their wanderings and basically move as the cone crop varies. In eastern regions several winters may pass before an influx occurs. When it does come it often seems that the distinct *jip–jip–jip* notes of the roaming flocks can be heard everywhere. They are often fond of saltings and gravelling at the roadside and little swirls can be seen flying up as one passes. Note the female's yellow rump;

FACTS AND FEATURES

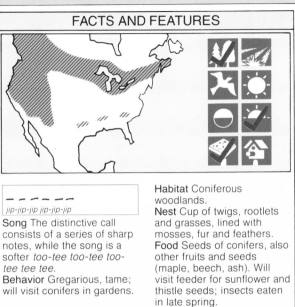

jip-jip-jip jip-jip-jip

Song The distinctive call consists of a series of sharp notes, while the song is a softer *too-tee too-tee too-tee tee tee.*
Behavior Gregarious, tame; will visit conifers in gardens.

Habitat Coniferous woodlands.
Nest Cup of twigs, rootlets and grasses, lined with mosses, fur and feathers.
Food Seeds of conifers, also other fruits and seeds (maple, beech, ash). Will visit feeder for sunflower and thistle seeds; insects eaten in late spring.

this is very distinctive and the best key when there is a group of females and immature. Also, arrivals from the north are often unbelievably tame allowing one to approach very close, up to a few inches. At banding operations I have actually picked birds off the limbs of trees to band them! At the feeding tray sunflower seeds will disappear quickly. But enjoy the birds, they may not be back for a very long time.

This bird's distinctive crossed bill enables it to open pine cones and extract the seed inside. It lives in coniferous forests across Canada, in the mountains in the western part of the United States and in northern Mexico. When the seed and cone crops there fail, it may move into other coniferous areas. Length 6½ inches

PINE SISKIN *Carduelis pinus*

AS THE LEAVES OF FALL take on their multicolored hues throughout the East, the crisp air not only carries forewarnings of the onset of winter but also the high pitched *sweeee – sweeee – ji-ji-jit – sweee* of the first Pine Siskins. Often they will be seen in small groups bobbing along in the characteristic flight of the goldfinch family. They rise and fall in this undulating pattern then quickly swing around and plummet downward, landing in the treetops. More often than not they have been attracted to a tree with catkin-type fruit such as an alder or birch. Trim birds, they are heavily marked with dark brown streaking. The wings show distinct yellowish wing bars, with yellow also on the sides of the short tail. The bill is very slim and dark. It is this feature that separates them from the other groups of heavier billed finches. In the tree they work quickly hanging about from the fruiting structures like ornaments on a tree. Using their thin bill to manipulate the catkins a shower of shucked parts filters from the tree. Then, as if a silent signal had been given, they explode from the treetop and are gone from sight.

The feeding tray will soon play host to these winter invaders. Their favorite food without question is thistle seed. A thistle-seed feeder will be emptied rapidly as a progression of birds occupy the pegs of the feeder throughout the day. Other seeds will be taken while birds wait their turn for the choicest morsels.

The number of siskins reaching the southern edge of their range varies greatly. During some winters thousands will be seen. Such invasion years often lead

FACTS AND FEATURES

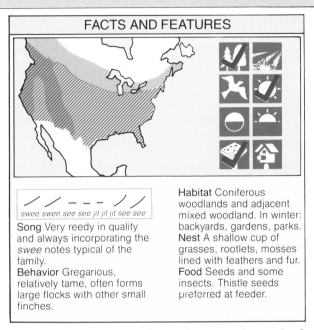

swee swee see see jit jit jit see see

Song Very reedy in quality and always incorporating the *swee* notes typical of the family.
Behavior Gregarious, relatively tame, often forms large flocks with other small finches.

Habitat Coniferous woodlands and adjacent mixed woodland. In winter: backyards, gardens, parks.
Nest A shallow cup of grasses, rootlets, mosses lined with feathers and fur.
Food Seeds and some insects. Thistle seeds preferred at feeder.

to residual populations that at times nest far south of their normal nesting range. In the western portion of North America the mountainous areas and high plateaus host the species year-round.

As the signs of spring appear some birds linger at feeders well on into May reluctant to depart from their constant food supply. But finally the urge to nest takes over and once again the journey south begins.

Similar to the goldfinch in appearance and song, the Pine Siskin makes its home in woodland, garden or park. The species is relatively tame. Length 5 inches

PURPLE FINCH *Carpodacus purpureus*

IF EVER THERE WAS A MISNOMER in identifying a bird by its name, this is one; "wine-colored" or "raspberry finch" would be much more fitting, but certainly not "purple." In coloration the male is distinct in its wine-colored plumage that is washed with this color throughout. Note that there are none of the brown lines on the side that one sees in a house finch. The female is more sparrow-like but has heavy streaking and a very distinct line over the eye contrasting to the deep chocolate brown cap.

The song is a clear musical jumble of notes that invariably ends with the *too—eee* sound that from a distance sounds a bit like a towhee.

This bird has an interesting range in that it is a permanent resident on the East and West coasts with the whole population linking up via a wide band of summer birds across Canada. It is from this population that tremendous numbers migrate on their way to the southern United States in the fall. Their call note during migration is a distinct *tick* or *tick-tick*; once learned this not only aids in identification of flying birds but also is the first indication that the birds are present in the nearby woodlands. They have a wide range of habitat preference ranging from evergreen forests to mixed upland woods, orchards, parklands and on into the backyards of suburbia.

During the winter months it will often be seen at a

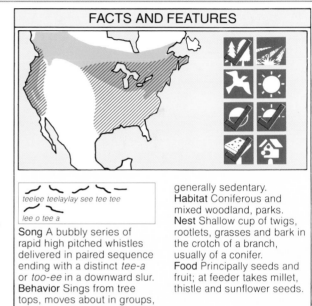

FACTS AND FEATURES

teelee teelaylay see tee tee

lee o tee a

Song A bubbly series of rapid high pitched whistles delivered in paired sequence ending with a distinct *tee-a* or *too-ee* in a downward slur.
Behavior Sings from tree tops, moves about in groups, generally sedentary.
Habitat Coniferous and mixed woodland, parks.
Nest Shallow cup of twigs, rootlets, grasses and bark in the crotch of a branch, usually of a conifer.
Food Principally seeds and fruit; at feeder takes millet, thistle and sunflower seeds.

feeder cracking sunflower seeds with its large powerful bill. Very aggressive at the feeder site, a Purple Finch will take control for hours and easily put a dent into the day's food supplies.

The "country cousin" of the house finch and often confused with it, the purple finch is larger, and the male is washed over most of its body with a rosy red color. The female is brown and heavily streaked. Length 6 inches

RUSTY BLACKBIRD *Euphagus carolinus*

The rust colored tips on the back and wing feathers that give this bird its name appear only in the fall. During the breeding season, the male has a glossy back plumage, legs and bill. The rusty blackbird lives in bogs, damp woodlands and swamps. Length 9 inches

FACTS AND FEATURES

chack chack chack/kish-lay

Song A short repeated rattle-like call; song is harsh and squeaky.
Behavior Walks about in wet areas turning over leaves for food.
Habitat Almost always near water, boggy edges of northern coniferous woods.
Nest Bulky cup of grasses and twigs often in willow or alder.
Food Insects and their larvae, spiders, seeds and berries. Will visit feeder for seeds with other blackbird flocks.

OF ALL THE MEMBERS of the blackbird family that inhabit North America, the Rusty is the most northerly breeding species. Outside of a small area in northern New England, Rusties appear in the lower 48 states only during the migration period and the winter. Indeed, many people overlook this species as it often blends in with the other large flocks of blackbirds moving about at this time.

Habitat is an excellent key to locating the Rusty Blackbird as it prefers wet swampy edges, boggy areas and brooklets. Here it walks slowly probing the grasses and flipping over leaves in a search for insects, worms and other invertebrates. The thickets that surround cattail marshes with their associated tangles of alder are a prime location habitat in which to locate this handsome blackbird. Approaching such an area the birder is usually greeted by several loud *chack*, *chack* notes, and a handful of birds pop into view to inspect the intruder.

In breeding plumage they are a uniform muted black with a pure yellow iris: the iris color is a consistent feature for all plumages. The color of the fall plumage gives the bird its name, with the feather edges showing a rich, coppery-rust color. Often the nape and back take on a more solid copper hue. At this time, too, the face shows a distinct eyeline and cheek mark, and also note the rounded appearance of the tail-tip.

In the spring and fall the song may be heard, a raspy, creaking *kish – a – lee* often described as a hinge badly in need of oil. They depart early in the spring for their northern tree-line nesting grounds, sometimes venturing into the bog areas of open tundra with its stunted vegetation. Again, wetland areas are the preferred habitat. The bulky cup of twigs, sedges and lichens is often placed in a conifer but at times necessity dictates that it is placed within a foot of the ground in a stunted tree or shrub.

RED-WINGED BLACKBIRD *Agelaius phoeniceus*

A SPECIES FAMILIAR to almost everyone, birder or otherwise, across the United States, it is certainly one of the handful of birds that children learn in their first years at school. At last, a bird whose name actually describes its markings – a redwinged black bird!

Perched atop a cattail in marshes from coast to coast the familiar *conk–ca–ree* is the sound one most often associates with this habitat. It is a most interesting species and one that has been studied in depth. It tends to have two basic territories. The nesting territory is defended with reckless abandon by the male. From its song perch with vermillion epaulets flashing it pursues any stray male that crosses the invisible line of demarcation. And it has a lot to defend, because it is a polygamous species, one male maintaining several nesting females. The other territory is a feeding area which is less strongly guarded against other intruding male birds.

The females look more like large sparrows than blackbirds. Heavily streaked with yellowish or orange tinting to the facial area, they arrive on the nesting territory a couple of weeks later than the males who have gone on in advance to set up their selected sites.

The species is represented by individuals throughout their entire range – except in the far north – in all months of the year. However, a substantial portion of the population does migrate south and this spells havoc for some southern roost areas. Populations in some states can exceed 11 million birds in a fairly small area and have caused health hazards – not to mention the noise factor. Dramatic steps have been taken to disturb such roosts but in general no great inroads have been made in population reduction. Known as crop thieves they can cause considerable damage at key times in crop development with disastrous attacks on grain fields, especially in the West, and rice fields in the South. A great deal of time, money and effort has been put forward to learn how to manage the species, often with little result.

But for most, it remains a sure sign of spring. The early arriving flocks from the South calling in loud cacophony from the tops of trees in the heart of towns signal to all that winter will soon be gone. Soon territories are established and the familiar cry of *conk–a–ree* echoes over the marsh.

FACTS AND FEATURES

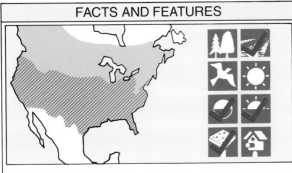

conk-a ree conk-a ree

Song Loud, short and ringing with the ending drawn out.
Behavior Polygamous; forms massive feeding flocks in the fall and winter.
Habitat Cattail marshes, upland grassland, wood edge, dry fields.
Nest A cup of grasses, plant fibers and bark strips. Placed in grass tussock, woven into marsh vegetation or in crotch of scrub trees.
Food Insects, invertebrates and a wide range of seeds. In cornfields damages newly formed cobs; at feeding tray cracked corn is a favorite.

In winter, this bird is a likely visitor to any birdfeeder. The male's bright red shoulder patches with pale yellow edging make it easy to identify in flight, but they may not be as visible when it is perched. The female is brown above and heavily streaked on the underside. Length 8¾ inches

YELLOW-HEADED BLACKBIRD *Xanthocephalus xanthocephalus*

Its black body, yellow head and breast and white wing patches make this bird unmistakable. The female is small and lacks the wing patch, but it can be identified by its yellow breast streaked with white at the lower end. Yellow-headed blackbirds live in marshes and feed in grain fields. Length 9½ inches

ALONG THE REEDY EDGES of freshwater lakes in western regions the spring air is filled with sounds that seem more electronic than those of a bird. These squeaks and wheezes, much like the static on an old radio, are produced by one of the handsomest of the blackbirds. Its name adequately describes its salient features: a yellow-headed black bird. A large bird, all plumages from juvenile through female and first winter males show the same gold-yellow to the head and throat region. But it is the male in breeding plumage that has the full hood, with black wings that flash bold white rectangles in the wing coverts. A highly gregarious species throughout the year the nesting marshes often harbor huge nesting colonies and the din created by the singing males can almost be overwhelming. Rather than foraging only in the marsh for food they spread out over nearby agricultural land and mass in large flocks.

At the end of the breeding season they group with other blackbirds and concentrate in massive build ups in agricultural lands and pastures farther south, from southern California and the Mexican border through to Texas. Very often these flocks consist only of winter plumage males and young males, the major portion of females wintering farther south in Mexico.

Every year birds stray to the East coast where they delight the birder who is diligent enough to search through the massive wintering flocks of blackbirds. In some instances the birds will join blackbirds that come to feeders for seeds or any other form of handout. Cracked corn is taken readily. The predominance of eastern sightings have been from diligent feeder watchers that meet with this dramatic blackbird for the first time at the feeder site.

FACTS AND FEATURES

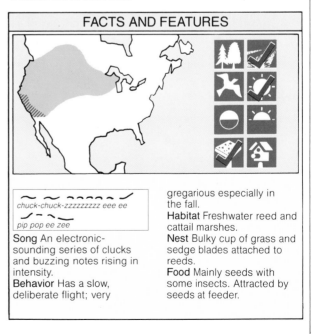

chuck-chuck-zzzzzzzzzz eee ee

pip pop ee zee

Song An electronic-sounding series of clucks and buzzing notes rising in intensity.
Behavior Has a slow, deliberate flight; very gregarious especially in the fall.
Habitat Freshwater reed and cattail marshes.
Nest Bulky cup of grass and sedge blades attached to reeds.
Food Mainly seeds with some insects. Attracted by seeds at feeder.

BOBOLINK *Dolichonyx oryzivorus*

WHEN I WAS A BOY some of my happiest birding times were spent with the birds of the waving grasslands. I would position myself in the deep grasses and from this emerald pocket watch as the Bobolink sailed past on stiffened wings singing their jumbled series of metallic notes. They would land atop tufts of alfalfa and sing for hours on end, sallying off in aerial flight song or in dashing pursuit of the yellowish-brown female. The Bobolink's color pattern appears to be upside-down in its orientation. Black underbelly contrasts sharply to the white of the shoulder, back and rump and the rich yellow at the nape of the neck. In full song with head thrown back the puffed yellow feathers of the nape makes the head look exceptionally large. The song has been interpreted in many ways, from *bob–o–link* to *link–link–Lincoln*. Its metallic quality and jumbled notes once heard are easily remembered.

Though finding and studying the bird was fairly simple, locating the nest turned out to be a major task. I spent days watching the females plunge into the deep grasses with food and though I worked the areas – no nest. After days of search I flushed one from directly at my feet. The nest, made of grasses, was tucked well into the grasses' overlapping bases and leading away was an obvious runway. The female lands and sneaks a significant distance to the nest. The eggs are reddish brown splotched with a rich reddish purple.

In the fall the males assume the same yellowish buff

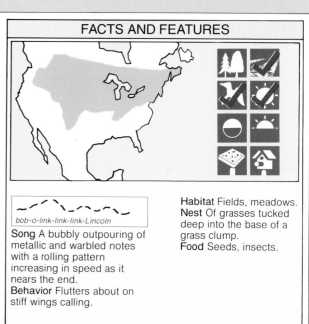

FACTS AND FEATURES

bob-o-link-link-link-Lincoln

Song A bubbly outpouring of metallic and warbled notes with a rolling pattern increasing in speed as it nears the end.
Behavior Flutters about on stiff wings calling.

Habitat Fields, meadows.
Nest Of grasses tucked deep into the base of a grass clump.
Food Seeds, insects.

color of the females and head for Latin America. On fall mornings thousands can be heard as they pass overhead giving their distinctive *pink–pink–pink* call notes. In May they will return to the rolling grasslands and afford others the joy I knew as a boy and still feel when I pass the spring meadows.

A familiar bird in fields and meadows in summer, the bobolink may also be found in marshes during its fall migration. The breeding male has black underparts, a tan nape and white rump with white feathers at the base of its wings. The tail feathers of both male and female narrow to sharp points. The male often sings a bubbling song on the wing. Length 7 inches

EASTERN MEADOWLARK *Sturnella magna*

NO SOUND BRINGS BACK birding memories of the fields and grasslands of North America as fast as the clear, two-parted song of the meadowlark. The sweet, liquid song is delivered most often from high up in a tree at the edge of a field, from the top of a small bush in an overgrown weedy field. With head thrown back, the brilliance of the yellow chest catches the sunlight and appears to glow. The broad, black chest V in striking contrast to the yellow, is actually a disruptive color pattern that aids in the bird's camouflage. When seen from the back the straw-brown and black streaking makes the bird virtually impossible to see in the grass.

Crossing a field, more often than not the first sighting will be birds jumping into flight near to the birder, flashing the white edges of their outer tail feathers as they scale off on stiff wingbeats uttering a rapid, metallic *bzzzeet* series of notes. Finding the nest of this species can be a challenge. After hours of searching, my first find came when the bird flushed literally from under my feet. I was so disoriented that it still took me some time to locate the cup of grass tucked deep into the bases of tangled grasses. Though it may not look like a member of the blackbird family, when seen walking deliberately about, probing under objects with its stocky bill, one can see why it has been placed in that group.

The Eastern Meadowlark is stockier, lacks yellow on the feathers at the base of the lower mandible and prefers a moister habitat than its look-alike western cousin of the dry grass plains.

With its dull brown back pattern, the meadowlark is well camouflaged while it forages for insects in the grasslands where it lives. In winter, it may add grains and fallen fruit to its diet. Length 10 inches

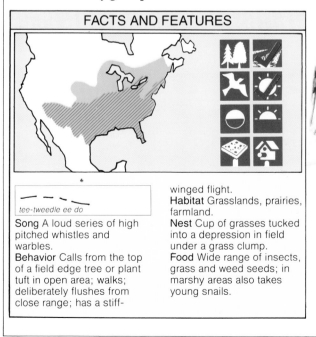

FACTS AND FEATURES

tee-tweedle ee do

Song A loud series of high pitched whistles and warbles.
Behavior Calls from the top of a field edge tree or plant tuft in open area; walks; deliberately flushes from close range; has a stiff-winged flight.
Habitat Grasslands, prairies, farmland.
Nest Cup of grasses tucked into a depression in field under a grass clump.
Food Wide range of insects, grass and weed seeds; in marshy areas also takes young snails.

NORTHERN ORIOLE *Icterus galbula*

TO MANY BIRDERS it was a near impossible task. To use the name "Northern" in place of "Baltimore" or "Bullock's Oriole" was a retraining to which many still fail to adjust. In the lush gallery forests along the major rivers crossing this extensive grassland of the Great Plains, the territories of the Baltimore and Bullock's Orioles overlap. Within this overlap the two species breed freely, forming hybrids that showed features of both. Based on this the two became one and were then termed the Northern Oriole. Be it Northern, Baltimore or Bullock's they remain one of the more familiar birds of the blackbird family. Blackbirds! But they are a magnificent orange and black – colorful members of the family most consider to be dull-plume birds.

This is another species that has learned to live well

The distinctive orange and black of the male is easy to spot, but the female is often confused with other species. It can be distinguished by its deep yellow-orange breast. Its two wing bars separate it from all but the western tanager. Length 8½ inches

A Baltimore oriole feeds its young housed in a woven, hanging nest slung between outer tree branches. Baltimore orioles incorporate threads and yarn into their nest and prefer white yarn or twine to any other colors

with man. Enjoying the large shade trees that line the streets and are found in backyards the Northern Oriole has taken up residence. It is often not until winter comes and leaves fall that one finally learns the whereabouts of the nest that was tended throughout the summer but was impossible to locate. Suspended from the very tip of a high swaying branch will be the gray elongated pouch that is diagnostic for this species. Made of plant fibers and grasses it provides the perfect cradle for the young as they sway back and forth even in the gentlest of breezes. Not only does the Oriole bring us pleasure with its bright colors, its song is a mellow whistle delivered from the highest tree tops before it darts off in a flash of color giving off a series of loud *check–check–check* notes which gives away its blackbird background.

In addition to enriching our lives with color and song they also are most beneficial as they feed on destructive insects. These include the hairy caterpillars of serious pests such as the tent moth caterpillar, taken with relish by this species but rejected by most other birds.

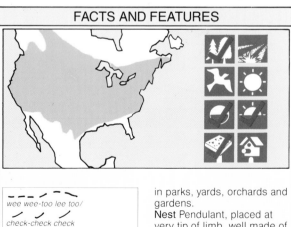

FACTS AND FEATURES

wee wee-too lee too/
check-check check

Song Introduced by clear whistles followed by a triplet of short whistled phrases; call is harsh and rapid.
Habitat Open woodlands, riverine forest, shade trees in parks, yards, orchards and gardens.
Nest Pendulant, placed at very tip of limb, well made of grasses and plant fibers.
Food Principally insects including hairy caterpillars, with some fruit and seeds; fruits taken in winter, when it will also take suet at feeder.

ORCHARD ORIOLE *Icterus spurius*

IT ALWAYS SEEMS to come as a surprise to people when they learn that orioles are members of the blackbird family. Certainly they are among the most colorful of the group. The Orchard Oriole male has beautiful chestnut plumage at maturity with a black hood and cowl. In its first year it is more the typical oriole in color being a lemon-yellow with black face and bib. It is the smallest North American oriole, a shade over 7in in length and very trim in stature.

In many areas this bird has become the oriole of tree-lined streets and parks and like the other orioles, stream-side shaded groves are another favored haunt. The Orchard Oriole is a gregarious species, nesting in loose colonies. One Louisiana study showed over 100 nests in a seven-acre study plot. The nest is a shallow cup of woven fibers placed in the fork of a limb but not nearly as pendulant as a northern oriole's. The bottom of the nest is often packed with a dense matting of plant down. Should a nest site be set up along a neighborhood street, the birder is in store for delightful singing from spring and early summer. The song is made up of loud, clear whistled notes, bubbling runs of cascading slurs, and metallic notes often ending or introduced by a clear phrasing of *what–cheer*.

This is a species that will adapt readily to a garden setting, and if twine or string is placed out in short strands from a hanging mesh basket they will often

FACTS AND FEATURES

what-cheer-kalee kalee-tolee

tolee-tolay what-cheer

Song A rolling bubbly series introduced or ending with a distinctive *what-cheer.*
Behavior Sociable, nests in loose colonies, often hangs head downward.
Habitat Shade trees, orchards, riverine forest, open woodland, parks.
Nest A shallow cup of woven dried grasses and plant fibers suspended in fork of outer limb, usually of fruit tree.
Food Mainly insects, spiders, some berries and seeds. Attracted to feeder by water.

come repeatedly to gather this material for nesting. I have also had excellent luck with masses of old cattail head "down." Availability of water in a bath is another most desirable garden feature that will attract all types of oriole.

For the first year of its life, the male is a yellow-green like the female, but it then turns a deep chestnut and gains a jet black hood. Orchard orioles live in city parks, gardens and orchards and build their nests in shade trees. They eat mainly insects, spiders and other invertebrates. Length 7 inches

SUMMER TANAGER *Piranga rubra*

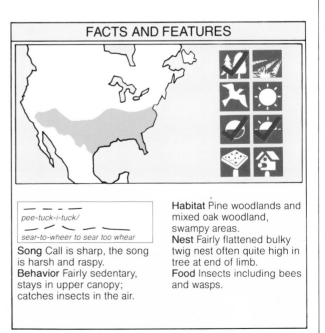

Numerous in oak-pine woodlands and in cottonwoods. The male has mottled green-red plumage during its first spring and then turns red. Females are usually yellow-green above and a dull yellow below, but some are a dull red color. Length 7½ inches

PEE – TUCK – I – TUCK is a common sound of southern mixed oak and pine woodland. Once this call note is learned, the birder becomes aware of how widespread this species can be. Hopping into view it stands out like a glowing red light against the lush green foliage. The male is all red with a large yellowish bill; the female, an orange-yellow throughout, lacking the dark wings of the greener scarlet tanager with which it might be confused. With slow and deliberate movements these orioles work the lower canopy of trees for insects, stopping, peering and then grabbing at a morsel.

This species really has a two-parted lifestyle. In the East they tend to be smaller and like oak-pine woodlands, whereas the western population prefer to live by water courses and cottonwood thickets, and tend to be larger. Recent bird censuses have shown a slow withdrawal of the northern limits of the eastern nesting range. Though certainly not a feeder species, birds out of their normal range lingering in the North will often revert to feeders for food to help them make it through the winter. I have spent many days at a kitchen window in the Northeast watching a Summer Tanager feeding on suet, orange halves and sunflower seeds while the snow of a December storm swirled in. This is a far cry from the bird's normal winter ground of Mexico and Central America. Tanagers as a group are a neotropical species that fortunately for us have extended their range slowly northwards.

FACTS AND FEATURES

pee-tuck-i-tuck/

sear-to-wheer to sear too whear

Song Call is sharp, the song is harsh and raspy.
Behavior Fairly sedentary, stays in upper canopy; catches insects in the air.

Habitat Pine woodlands and mixed oak woodland, swampy areas.
Nest Fairly flattened bulky twig nest often quite high in tree at end of limb.
Food Insects including bees and wasps.

WESTERN TANAGER *Piranga ludoviciana*

The western tanager's wing bars distinguish it from other birds. The upper bar is usually a brighter yellow than the lower. The male has a red head which turns yellow-green in the fall, also, yellow underparts, collar and rump and black back, wings and tail. It lives in coniferous forests. Length 7¼ inches

THE STRIKING BEAUTY OF AN ADULT male Western Tanager is difficult to surpass, as it appears at the edge of a deep green coniferous tree limb. For such sightings adjectives alone do not suffice, only the inner feeling one gets during those special moments afield will hold the imprint.

As the name implies this is a truly western bird. Its haunts are the open coniferous forests of both mountains and coastal lowlands. In such areas as the birder wanders through the still forests, the strong call note is commonly heard – *prid-it prid-it*, a clue that this sedentary bird is high above in the canopy. If the female is seen she might be mistaken at first for a female oriole, but the heavier bill, darker upper parts and pale cheeks make them easy to distinguish from each other. The nest will be placed very high in the tree on a flattened portion of limb and branch and is a simple cup of twigs.

Normally the species winters in Mexico and farther south. However, some birds stay as far north as Oregon, and others wander in an easterly direction and wind up on the East Coast. During such wanderings or while in migration these birds do show up in gardens or at the feeding tray. Fruit is taken readily and cut-up orange halves with great delight. In the woodlands cascara berries prove to be the most favored plant during migration. At these times willow thickets and oak bottomlands should be checked as the birds make their way south of the border.

FACTS AND FEATURES

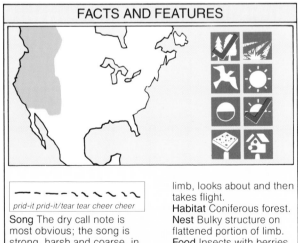

prid-it prid-it/tear tear cheer cheer

Song The dry call note is most obvious; the song is strong, harsh and coarse, in a two part sequence.
Behavior Sedentary, moves about slowly in trees. Often comes to outer portion of limb, looks about and then takes flight.
Habitat Coniferous forest.
Nest Bulky structure on flattened portion of limb.
Food Insects with berries later in the season.

SCARLET TANAGER *Piranga olivacea*

IT IS ALWAYS A DELIGHT, to walk in the awakening upland forests of the Northeast in springtime with the subtle greens of unfolding leaves and the Japanese-like tracery of the flattened bows of dogwood trees forming the understory. Add to this the brilliance of a male Scarlet Tanager hopping into view and one's breath is nearly taken away! The brilliant red of the body sharply contrasts with the jet black of the wings and tail making it one of the most striking North American birds to be found. The female is a lemon yellow with olive wings and a black button of an eye.

Tanagers can seem lethargic in their movements and are often overlooked as they move about feeding in the full-foliaged canopy. For this reason they are thought of as much rarer than they actually are. One way to get a true feeling of how common they are is to learn their diagnostic song. It is a raspy, harsh *hurry, to worry, flurry, its blurry*. As diagnostic is the harsh call note *chip – burr*.

The nest is usually placed fairly high in a tree and in the fork of a branch way out on the end of a limb – a most inaccessible place. This is unfortunate as the eggs are a beautiful greenish-blue with fine spotting of chestnut, purplish and lilac.

In the winter the Scarlet Tanager heads for South America and early spring sees their return. Unfortunately their timing can be a bit premature, and at this time, spectacular build-ups of birds at the moderating

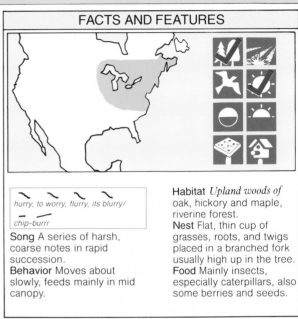

FACTS AND FEATURES

hurry, to worry, flurry, its blurry/

chip-burrr

Song A series of harsh, coarse notes in rapid succession.
Behavior Moves about slowly, feeds mainly in mid canopy.

Habitat *Upland woods of* oak, hickory and maple, riverine forest.
Nest Flat, thin cup of grasses, roots, and twigs placed in a branched fork usually high up in the tree.
Food Mainly insects, especially caterpillars, also some berries and seeds.

coast habitats cover the ground and every tree. I have seen dozens huddled in the road or along the beach rack-line looking for insects. Some will perish but most will survive to again punctuate the spring woods with embers of glowing color, the highlight of a birder's morning.

The male is bright red; its black wing and tail distinguish it from the summer tanager. The female is olive green above and green-yellow underneath with a smaller, darker bill than the female summer tanager. Scarlet tanagers live in deciduous and mixed woodlands. Length 7 inches

USEFUL ADDRESSES

US

American Birding Association
PO Box 4335
Austin
TX 78765

American Ornithologists Union
National Museum of Natural
History
Smithsonian Institution
Washington
DC 20560

Cooper Ornithological Society
Dept of Biology
University of California
Los Angeles
CA 90024

**Cornell University Laboratory
of Ornithology**
159 Sapsucker Woods Road
Ithaca
NY 14853

National Audubon Society
950 Third Avenue
New York
NY 10022

National Wildlife Federation
1412 16th Street
NW
Washington
DC 20036

Nature Society
Purple Martin Junction
Griggsville
IL 62340

**North American Bluebird
Society**
PO Box 6295
Silver Spring
MD 20906

Wilson Ornithological Society
c/o Josselyn Van Tyne Memorial
Library
Museum of Zoology
University of Michigan
Ann Arbor
MI 48104

CANADA

Canadian Nature Federation
Suite 203
75 Albert Street
Ottawa
K1P 6G1

AUSTRALIA

**Royal Australian
Ornithologists Union**
21 Gladstone Street,
Moonee Ponds
Victoria 3039

BRITAIN

British Ornithologists Union
c/o Zoological Society of London
Regent's Park
London NW1 4BX

International Council for Bird Preservation
219c Huntingdon Road
Cambridge
CB3 0DL

Oriental Bird Club
c/o The Lodge
Sandy
Bedfordshire
SG19 2DL

Ornithological Society of the Middle East
c/o The Lodge
Sandy
Bedfordshire
SG19 2DL

INDIA

Bombay Natural History Society
Hornbill House
Shadid Bhagat Singh Road
Bombay 400 023

JAPAN

Wild Bird Society of Japan
Aoyama Building
1-1-4 Shibuya
Shibuya-ka
Tokyo 150

SCANDINAVIA

Scandinavian Ornithologists Union
Dept of Animal Ecology
Ecology Building
S-223 62 Lund

AFRICA

East Africa Natural History Society
Ornithological Committee
Box 48019
Nairobi
KENYA

South African Ornithological Society
PO Box 87234
Houghton
Johannesburg 2041
SOUTH AFRICA

INDEX

Credits
Photographs by kind permission of the Frank Lane Agency. Pages *6-51*, illustrations by Vana Haggerty; pages *52-155*, illustrations by David Ord Kerr.